The Creative Copycat

THE CREATIVE COPYCAT

MARIAN L. CANOLES

Illustrations
by
Kelly Royall

LIBRARIES UNLIMITED, INC.

Littleton, Colorado   **1982**

LIBRARIES UNLIMITED, INC.
P. O. Box 263
Littleton, Colorado 80160

Library of Congress Cataloging in Publication Data

Canoles, Marian L., 1927-
    The creative copycat.

    Bibliography: p. 251
    Includes index.
    1. Bulletin boards--Handbooks, manuals, etc.
I. Title.
LB1043.58.C36   371.3'356   82-15329
ISBN 0-87287-340-4   AACR2

Libraries Unlimited books are bound with Type II nonwoven material that meets and
exceeds National Association of State Textbook Administrators' Type II nonwoven
material specifications Class A through E.

FOREWORD
By Richard Armour

Here is a book that should give both enjoyment and help to librarians who wish to exhibit eye-catching and reader-catching displays.

Marian Canoles does all users of libraries a great service by providing them with display ideas month by month through the year, noting the seasons and holidays as well as the sometimes overlooked kinds of reading available.

The illustrations by Kelly Royall add an element of fun to the book and also make it possible, when used with the instructions, for even the least mechanically skilled person to construct the displays. I feel I could even do it myself.

As one whose second home is a library and who is aware of the importance of displays in bringing books and readers together, I am sure that not only librarians but teachers will benefit from this inventive and delightfully readable book.

5

TABLE OF CONTENTS

INTRODUCTION

"There's so much in the world to know. How can I ever learn it all?"
I was eleven years old.

"You can't master everything, child," my father replied, *"the secret lies not in how much you know, but in your ability to know how to find the answers."* Thirty years later, when I entered a career in library service, I recalled my father's words more as prophecy than aphorism. Helping young people to find information was a wholly fulfilling occupation.

One aspect of library work came as a bit of a surprise, however. I was in no way prepared to fill the need for creating bulletin board displays, attributable to a singular lack of artistic talent. Nevertheless, in my apprentice days, this task fell to me. The overworked librarian-in-charge welcomed the relief of having someone else take over the job.

Just out of school, brimming with untapped energy, I tried hard to do my best. I pored over each display, longing to create something original — something that would cause people to stop, look, and react. From the start, therefore, my chosen theme was the eccentric—the offbeat.

One of my first displays was a Christmas board — a girl and boy looking through a window of clear plastic into the library; she with yellow yarn braids, and he in cap with tousled brown hair. I arranged black paper mullions over the plastic, forming small windows, then scattered bits of cotton (snow) over all, under the caption, "Waiting for Santa". I got the reaction I wanted. Everyone said, "How original!"

Deep down I knew it was not original—that I must have somewhere seen a picture that gave me the idea, a picture that I perceived would work on a bulletin board with bits of fabric, paper, cotton, and yarn. The fatherly wisdom of long ago applied not only academically, but artistically as well. Hereafter, I continued to adapt and rework professionally produced material to suit the needs of the school and public library, an effort that has culminated in this copycat collection of bulletin board display ideas.

You may think it presumptuous that one who makes no pretense of artistic ability would dare to assemble a book on this subject. I venture to do so, however, because I perceive that this same lack of skill is not uncommon among librarians, and that a different approach would be welcome.

The problem and burden of inventing new displays regularly can be a grinding chore over the years — a nagging worry when you are responsible for three or more presentations monthly, some in large windows, requiring a touch of the spectacular. Thus, librarians who plead ignorance of the elements and principles of design use this excuse to postpone or overlook an unpleasant task.

Does humorist Richard Armour unsettle you when he describes today's library displays as a "minor duty of some minor member of the library staff. . .troublesome. . .remain[ing] unchanged for six months or even a year"?[1] This jestful observation hints that somewhere along the line we may have lost sight of our priorities and sacrificed crucial communication to cash-fine collections.

The importance of attractive and provocative bulletin board displays cannot be overestimated. Display areas in and outside the library have high visibility and provide the librarian with a potentially powerful platform. Here you have an unprecedented advantage over other teachers and administrators. Hundreds of people pass by daily and the number of lives you may touch is legion. Your displays reflect the quality of the library, giving the viewer an overall impression of the place. You can provoke interest (or the opposite) in this initial overture to win friends and patrons.

Warmth, support, and understanding will generate from the unspoken word when you give each display the attention it deserves. For example, should you reproduce *Freedom of Speech* (page 81), using letters written by the students themselves, you will observe in their smiles and chatter a favorable response. The bulletin board display is a very special way of communicating, often far more effective than mere conversation.

Bulletin boards give you the opportunity to provoke thought, i.e., *What Next in Jerusalem?* (page 142); to advertise, *Six Ancient Machines* (page 38); and to reach out and grab passersby. *The Paperback Exchange* (page 37) was so popular with students and teachers that I was able to use it for an extended period. Visual display in celebration and commemoration of holidays is a good spot to add a new perspective (see *Hanukkah*, page 100).

The procedure I have followed solves the librarian's problem of developing creative displays, especially for those whose creativity skills are deficient. An unabashed copycat, I appropriate and adapt ideas conceived by professional artists and hucksters, often in a mix-and-match technique, and through the use of papercraft and inexpensive materials,

---

[1] Armour, Richard. *The Happy Bookers*. (New York: McGraw, 1976), p.6.

rework the layout to a unique end. I submit that any concept that can be drawn on paper can be given a new dimension with this method.

Displays in *The Creative Copycat* demonstrate this technique. Most are derived from the vast store of resources found in the library. All are based on eye-catching tricks of the advertising trade, processed to fit library goals. I have tried to give you what you need: an idea and a picture to go with it, with the underlying purpose of selling the public on books and reading. Only you can determine which displays best suit your needs.

Many boards can serve double-duty. The firecracker (page 244) for July 4th can be reused in a display on evolution vs. creation (the big-bang theory). Use Halloween masks (page 51) in a psychology board. The water safety board (page 233) can be adapted for use in a statement on pollution. The pulpit in the Martin Luther King display (page 105) for January can become the base of the gazebo in February's *The Game of Hearts* (page 138). The adaptability of the displays should be obvious, and possibilities are countless.

Most of these displays were executed within two frameworks: a window measuring 108"L by 34"D by 48"H and a board 70" by 47". Some displays lend themselves better to a large treatment in three dimensions. These can be simplified by you to serve in a less expansive area of two dimensions or in combination. For example, *The Power of the Printed Word* (page 131) looks best on an expansive background to avoid the confusion that can occur when newsprint is used for this purpose. The minor variation of reversing background and lettering (newsprint letters on a solid background) renders the display usable on a smaller scale.

The number of possible bulletin board ideas available to you is almost infinite. Ideas are delivered to your library door daily in the form of newspapers, magazines, books, and films, all teeming with possibilities. Look at everything: pictures (especially drawings), words and slogans, jokes, and all manner of advertising. Clip and catalog those materials that spark an idea. File these handily in a monthly arrangement for later adaptation.

Check the classifieds. Simple little drawings, enlarged, often make striking bulletin boards. Area magazines are a good source for local materials and often contain innovative advertising. Specialized magazines that have proliferated in the past decade, provide numerous useful ideas. Copy dramatic book covers. As new books arrive, make a note of art work that can be easily duplicated. Maps, calendars, illustrated brochures, and giveaways are plentiful and beg to be copied. Build around unusual items that come to hand. A teacher, married to a state legislator, once gave me a menu to a presidential dinner. Surely, there's a display in that item.

Whenever there are handouts, pick up two so you can mount the material front and back. In short, copy the advertisers boldly. They thrive in the workaday world. You, too, will thrive when you adapt their ideas, designed to achieve shallow goals, to accomplish a higher end. Your function is that of processor as you transform their ideas.

There are many reasons that support high expectations for success with this method, not the least of which is availability. Inquire at any library and you are apt to be told, "Sorry, all the bulletin board books are out—they stay out. We can't keep them on the shelves." With your own system you won't have to depend on others. Books go out of date, but your file will always be current. You can afford to discard items that seem dated because you are rich in ideas. In addition, you are always prepared because of the planning you have done in odd moments.

The cost of these boards is negligible. Colored construction paper and plastic letters are basic to all of the displays. Some items can be used repeatedly, such as fabric backgrounds, spreading the cost over years. Search remnant tables for interesting prints, i.e., camouflage for war or earth disaster; polka dots for circus life; and provincial prints, checks, plaids, and blue denim to offset themes of home and school. And what is cheaper than newsprint? Stock a variety of yarn, also. Invest in fake grass, plastic frames, colored clothespins and, perhaps, an easel. Certain materials can be obtained at a reduced rate when purchased at the end of season, i.e., tinsel garland after Christmas. With advanced planning, you can collect items you need well ahead of time.

It is by ingenious use of these materials that each display becomes yours alone and bears your personal imprint. Take a good look at your craft books and magazines for simple instructions on how to make almost anything. If you believe that all things are possible, you will be successful most of the time. More importantly, you will be altogether gratified by the discovery of a latent capability you never before thought you possessed.

During the months I worked on this book, I assumed that *I* was *The Creative Copycat*, processing tons of material clipped from magazines, newspapers, catalogs, and books to create these displays. Now I realize I am not it. The copycat is *you*. Your library gives you access to more information than you will ever need. You now know how to find it.

A young teacher, currently working on her doctorate, reminisced to me of her classroom days. The paramount truth she learned was, "Everything in teaching boils down to the personality of the teacher." This holds true for librarians as well. You put something of yourself into each display when you are creative. *You are your displays.* The idea may be pilfered, but your personality lies imprinted on each one, as if stamped with a mighty seal.

In this book, I have included a list of sources for materials as well as a bibliography of methods books that I hope you will find helpful as you assume the role of *Creative Copycat*. By planning ahead to create bulletin boards that are fresh and sparkling, you will begin to hear comments like, "Where do you get all your ideas? What will you do next?". More notably, you may hear one day, "I want to read a book I saw in your window. When can I have it?"

SEPTEMBER:

A FRESH START...

Life in P.S. 123...friendships...clubs...
a new beginning...30 days hath...
getting aquainted...apples...new
frontiers...teachers...ruledays...
reading...library services...writing...
equations...where am I?..what's
going on in the world?..Labor Day...
work...play...preparing for future...
LET'S HAVE A BALL...football...
new clothes...

LET'S GET THE SHOW ON THE ROAD!

−WELCOME BACK−

BACKGROUND: Blue denim fabric.

LETTERS: Large−red and white checked fabric (stiffen with iron-on interfacing). Cut out letters with pinking shears. Small−white plastic.

METHOD: Cut stars from light blue posterboard. Affix photos[1] of various faculty members to stars, and tack or hang stars to board.

---

[1] Ask at the Yearbook office for these; use with permission only.

–DESTINATION P. S. 123–

BACKGROUND: Green paper (or grass) below yellow brick road, blue above.

LETTERS: Cut out large letters from black construction paper squares. Print signs with black marker on white posterboard.

METHOD: Assemble a school bus with blocks of dark yellow posterboard. Use light yellow construction paper for a road. Offset signs with shredded green paper to resemble grass.

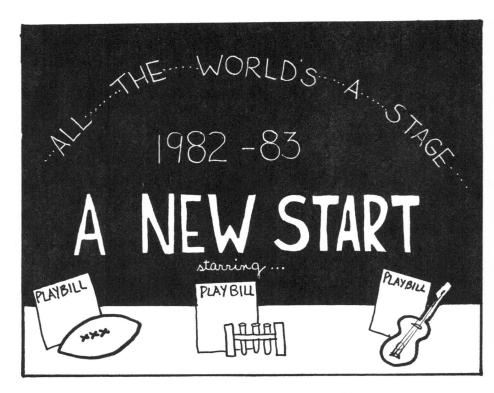

—ALL THE WORLD'S A STAGE—

BACKGROUND: Black construction paper or fabric.

LETTERS: Cut theme letters from white construction paper; cut numerals and play title from pastel paper. Write "starring" in white yarn.

METHOD: Tack theme lettering over an arc of gold sparkle garland. Playbills can be real or mock theater programs. Place on each program a picture or object that depicts a school activity.

−CLEAN SLATE−

BACKGROUND: Black paper or fabric.

LETTERS: With white chalk or yarn, make lines and write slogan.

METHOD: Hang an eraser and chalk with yarn or yellow measuring tape. Place suitable books nearby. Interesting bookends are useful here.

—WE'RE LOOKING FOR YOU—

BACKGROUND: Brown wrapping paper.

LETTERS: Dark brown cut-out and yarn.

METHOD: Use commercial animal posters, or make your own creation. (Primary coloring books are a good source for animal patterns.) Print librarians' names on paper medallions; hang on real or paper chains. Cut shrubbery in varicolored greens. Add blackbirds. For realistic effect, give giraffes lush felt eyelashes and a red felt tongue, with Easter grass spilling from their mouths.

—IN THE GAME OF LIFE—

BACKGROUND: Black and red checkerboard. Staple red squares over black paper or fabric background.

LETTERS: Large—white numerals cut from stencils. Small—white cut-out on black and red "men."

METHOD: Make checkers with jar caps covered with circles of red and black paper.

—ETC.—

BACKGROUND: Yellow paper.

LETTERS: Draw "ETC.'s" in oversized red marker, or cut from stencils. Print smaller lettering in blue marker.

METHOD: Use this easy display to call attention to new books and materials.

—IT'S CLASSIFIED—

BACKGROUND: Classified section of newspaper.

LETTERS: Commercial black plastic lettering for numerals and small lettering.

METHOD: Write classifications in red marker directly on newspaper background. Cut "IT'S CLASSIFIED" from white construction paper squares. Arrange on black posterboard base before tacking to board.

–BEST THINGS IN LIFE–

BACKGROUND: Any dark colored construction paper or fabric.

LETTERS: White–cut from stencils and blocks of white construction paper; commercial white plastic for very small print.

METHOD: Tack real audiovisual items to the board where possible. Book jackets can be taped over cardboard boxes for an in-depth effect. If a three-dimensional effect is desired, display with machines, i.e., filmloops and machine. Use clear plastic for television screen.

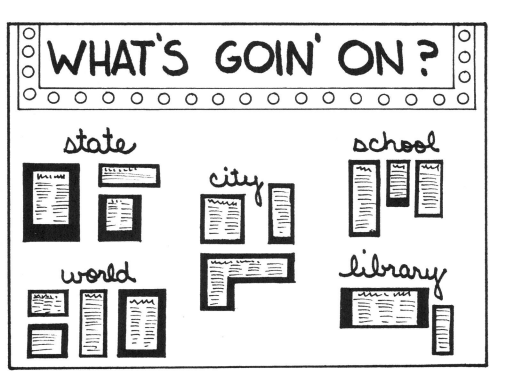

–WHAT'S GOIN' ON?–

BACKGROUND: Newsprint (avoid pictures).

LETTERS: Large–red cut-out. Script in oversized red marker.

METHOD: Mount worthy news items pertinent to each area on black construction paper. Create your own border arrangement to simulate a marquee.

—LAST GREAT FRONTIER—

BACKGROUND: Tan paper or fabric.

LETTERS: Large—orange on black cut-out. Small—black plastic.

METHOD: Display brain models (borrowed from your science department) on varisized boxes that have been covered with light and dark purple paper. Art reproductions by Dali, Picasso, and others may be obtained from your central office or cut from magazines and mounted by you. Display with psychology and biology books.

–LET'S HAVE A BALL–

BACKGROUND: Pink construction paper or fabric.

LETTERS: Write in red yarn or use paper cut-out lettering.

METHOD: Simulate a tuxedo by sketching in body lines around a real tie and cummerbund, or cut a tuxedo from black paper. The gown is shaped with velveteen bodice, sequined straps, and a gathered tulle skirt. Tie and suspend helium-filled balloons, which you may first decorate with tag lines.[1] Colored tissue puffs set off appropriate books. Sprinkle confetti and streamers over the board.

---

[1] See Purdy, Susan. *Holiday Cards for You to Make*, (Lippincott, 1967), p. 57.

−READING PLACE−

BACKGROUND: White paper.

LETTERS: Black cut-out.

METHOD: Cut apples from red construction paper. Make kelly green yarn pom-poms of diminishing size to depict the tail end of a worm.

−RETURN OF THE ONE-ARMED BANDIT−

BACKGROUND: Blue paper.

LETTERS: Large−black cut-out on red. Small−black plastic.

METHOD: Construct the Dewey with brown wrapping paper and decorate with varicolored construction paper and colored markers. Or, able library assistants should consider making fancy rendition of the Dewey. It would be an enjoyable project.

–EXTRA! EXTRA! EXTRA!–

BACKGROUND: Newsprint.

LETTERS: Use varying sizes of black felt markers, starting at the top line with giant size.

METHOD: This is an easy board where you do the printing. Use new, very wet markers; strokes must be bold to overpower newsprint. Tack on a list of your own bibliographies of new history books that can be found in your library, first mounting the lists on black or red construction paper.

−TEE OFF−

BACKGROUND: White paper.

LETTERS: Black cut-out.

METHOD: Apple, tee, golf green, and flag (with diploma) are made with red, green, and yellow construction paper. Roll a white paper diploma, and tie with a ribbon. The sign is of yellow posterboard, printed with green or black marker. For grass, make vertical cuts in strips of green tissue paper.

—UPS AND DOWNS OF READING—

BACKGROUND: Light blue paper or fabric.

LETTERS: Large—red yarn. Small—black plastic.

METHOD: Staple scaffolding of black posterboard strips. Make a track with straight pins and black yarn, narrowing it at the center of the board. Cover small lightweight boxes with varicolored construction paper. Insert one or two paperbacks in each box. Attach cars one to another with a chain.

—PAPERBACK EXCHANGE—

BACKGROUND: None.

LETTERS: Large—green cut-out. Small—black felt marker.

METHOD: This display is particularly well suited for a window arrangement. Make a shed roof of yellow corrugated paper. Print a sign on brown wrapping paper. Posts are two weather-beaten sticks anchored either on stands of clay or in buckets of sand/gravel. Add small antique items, i.e., milk can, tin crackerbox, coffee grinder, and a large assortment of used paperback books.

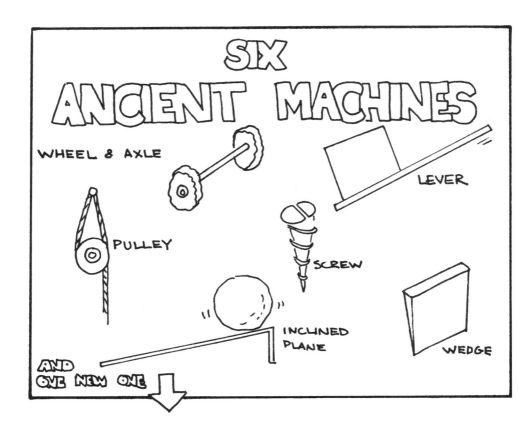

—SIX ANCIENT MACHINES—

BACKGROUND: Brown wrapping paper.

LETTERS: Large—black cut-out. Small—black plastic.

METHOD: Make very simple drawings of each machine, each on a different colored posterboard. Use this display to draw attention to your photocopying machine or a new piece of audiovisual equipment.

−THE CUSTOMER IS KING−

BACKGROUND: None.

LETTERS: Colored cut-out.

METHOD: Use a commercial animal poster here. Shred lots of green and brown construction paper and staple it about the animal's face to create a jungle.

OCTOBER:

LISTEN! THE WIND IS RISING...

Fall...leaves...nature...harvest...
Indian Summer...HALLOWEEN...
witchcraft...astrology...mythology...
philosophy...religion...mystery...man...
woman...animals...clean-up...
needlework...hobbies...reading...
tests...scholarships...

NOW FOR OCTOBER EVES...

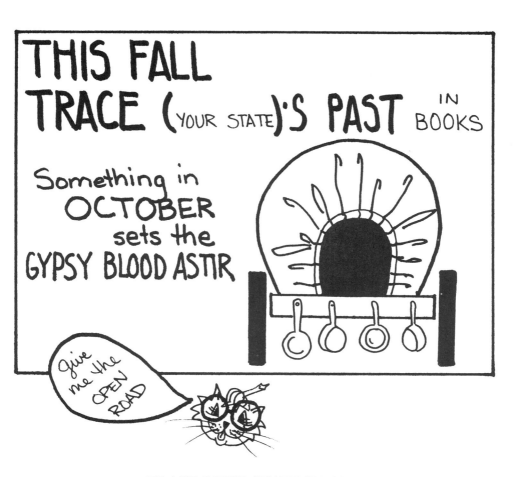

—TRACE (YOUR STATE)'S PAST—

BACKGROUND: None.

LETTERS: Large—black cut-out. Verses[1]—black plastic.

METHOD: Construct a wagon canopy with wire and unbleached muslin. Hang pots and pans on an axle made with posterboard or wood. Wheels are made with black posterboard.

---

[1] From *The Vagabond* by Bliss Carmen.

—BAGGING THE LEAVES—

BACKGROUND: Tan paper or fabric.

LETTERS: Black cut-out.

METHOD: Construct a fence with white posterboard slats. Cut green plastic garbage bags to a proportionate size, and fill with newspaper or straw. Add a farm hat, rake, and scarecrow if you have room.

—LOCAL COLOR—

BACKGROUND: Light blue paper.

LETTERS: Dark blue cut-out.

METHOD: Cut a tree trunk from brown construction paper; the foliage from red paper. Make a working color wheel for the center spot. The large individual leaves are cut from a variety of orange and yellow paper. Type or write book titles on each leaf.

—INDIAN SUMMER—

BACKGROUND: Orange paper or fabric.

LETTERS: Script—yellow and russet yarn. Small—black plastic.

METHOD: Frame Indian prints, purchased or cut from magazines, using inexpensive plexiglass frames. Add imitation leaves, cornstalks, and pumpkins. Display with Indian lore.

YOUR CHOICE

DON'T READ:

BE
A
PUPPET
ON
A
STRING

READ:

DON'T
BE
A
PUPPET
ON
A
STRING

—A CHOICE—

BACKGROUND: None.

LETTERS: Large—colored yarn or cut-out. Small—black plastic.

METHOD: Fashion a theater, using one or two shallow boxes. Gather the curtain on a rod (or string), and cover the heading with swags of the same fabric. Puppets can be real or made with paper dolls and string.

—BIG NIGHT—

BACKGROUND: Cover the area behind the pumpkin with black paper.

LETTERS: Black marker on white posterboard.

METHOD: Window shade, curtains, and cornice are done in a provincial print fabric. First, make the shade—stitch a casing, then insert a slat of wood or posterboard. Tack the shade flat across the top, and hang a yarn pull at the center. Second, gather fabric on a rod or string, and arrange it to hang on both sides of the board. Next, cover a posterboard cornice, and tack. Attach an orange pumpkin with paper "springs."

—ALL HALLOWS' EVE—

BACKGROUND: Imitation grass below horizon. Black construction paper above.

LETTERS: Large—black cut-out.

METHOD: Cut a house and barn from brown or charcoal paper. The moon is yellow. Cut out pumpkins and place the largest and shapliest ones in the foreground. Keep background pumpkins as attached segments.

—WHEN THE WORLD TURNS BLACK AND GOLD—

BACKGROUND: Gray fabric, preferably shiny acetate.

LETTERS: Large—metallic gift wrap, cut-out on black. Small—same paper (no black necessary on first part of slogan).

METHOD: Cut a window, bench, fireplace, and mantle from black posterboard. Construct a fire, moon, and moonlight with orange and yellow paper. Emphasize lines by edging with red and gold sparkle garland. Apply narrow gray strips for windowblinds. Cover corrugated candlesticks with gift wrap. Candles can be real or papermade. Group Halloween pictures over the mantle. Make a cat of black fur fabric or paper. Tack bits of sparkle for candle flames and cat's eyes.

—MURDER IN PRINT—

BACKGROUND: Newspaper.

LETTERS: Cut from white construction paper, edged with black marker.

METHOD: Cut large black footprints from construction paper. Dot drops of blood with a red marker. Display with a magnifying glass and Sherlock Holmes hat.

—GHOST STORIES—

BACKGROUND: Black paper or fabric.

LETTERS: Large—orange yarn. Small—white plastic.

METHOD: Fashion a ghost with white crepe paper. Encircle a purchased Halloween mask with paper. You may have to tie the ghost at the neck to allow the paper to fly fully and freely.

—DARE TO BE DIFFERENT—

BACKGROUND: Yellow paper.

LETTERS: Orange cut-out. Vary lettering style for the word "different."

METHOD: Make or buy a variety of Halloween masks. Obtain an official UNICEF box from your local chairman.

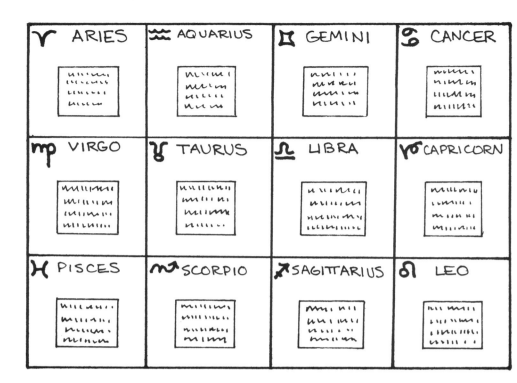

—ASTROLOGY BOARD—

BACKGROUND: White paper.

LETTERS: Signs and letters with felt pen.

METHOD: Type information for each sign,[1] and mount on varicolored construction paper. Laminate, if possible, for future use.

---

[1] For the 12 signs of the Zodiac, see *Merit Students Encyclopedia*, Vol. 2, (New York, NY: Macmillan, 1979), p. 320.

−GOOD VS. EVIL−

BACKGROUND: Sand construction paper.

LETTERS: Russet on black cut-out.

METHOD: A primitive style is basic to this display. Using a fine brush and brown tempera paint (or a large brown felt marker) paint a tree trunk and branches. Daub foliage, using a cotton ball and green ink pad. Cut russet apples from construction paper. Feature books on philosophy, psychology, or evolution vs. creation.

—DON'T GAMBLE—

BACKGROUND: Dark green paper or fabric.

LETTERS: Large/medium—white cut-out. Small—white plastic.

METHOD: Cover two boxes with shiny white wrapping paper. Glue black paper circles to each box surface. Use oversized playing cards for poker hands.

—READING THE BOOKS—

BACKGROUND: Yellow paper or fabric.

LETTERS: Black plastic.

METHOD: Make a light bulb with several layers of white tissue paper; edge with gold sparkle garland. Cover posterboard base with aluminum foil.

–GET MORE SATISFACTION–

BACKGROUND: An interesting fabric of your choice.

LETTERS: Large–cut-out. Small–black plastic.

METHOD: Use this display to promote oversized books, which are shelved separately in many libraries.

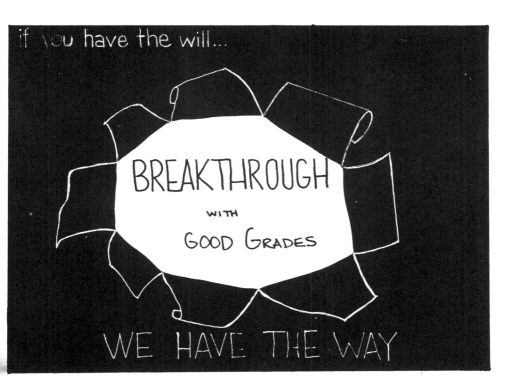

—BREAKTHROUGH—

BACKGROUND: Cover center area with white paper.

LETTERS: Inside the opening, the letters are black cut-out and black plastic. Outside the tear, letters are white.

METHOD: Cover the entire board with black paper (tar paper would be a good choice). Carefully tear back the paper, revealing the white center, and tack the edges to prevent sagging.

SCHOLARSHIPS

THE MOST EXPENSIVE HAT IN AMERICA
They are giving one away

–SCHOLARSHIPS–

BACKGROUND: White paper or fabric.

LETTERS: Large–black cut-out. Small–black plastic.

METHOD: Use a borrowed or purchased mortarboard. Tie a diploma with gold or yellow ribbon. Consult your Guidance Office for scholarship data to use with your display.

–PREPARE NOW–

BACKGROUND: None.

LETTERS: Yellow on orange cut-out.

METHOD: Fashion two bins from wire fencing. Fill one bin with real dried corn; the other with rolled diplomas tied with yellow ribbons. Box and save these diplomas to use in June in the *Big Payoff* board, on page 218.

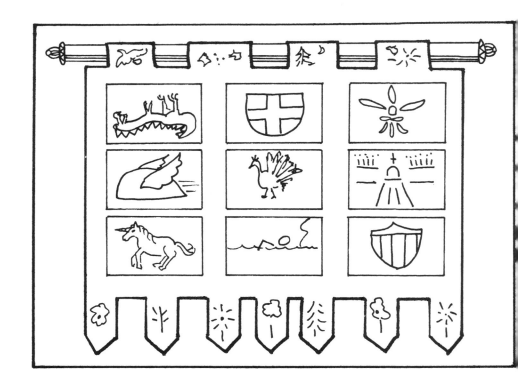

—TAPESTRY—

BACKGROUND: None.

LETTERS: None.

METHOD: This tapestry can be made with fabrics, colored felt, or construction paper. Mount the tapestry with scenes from myth and legend. Staple or pin the tapestry over a wooden dowel or brass curtain rod.

NOVEMBER:

THE LOVE OF BARE NOVEMBER DAYS...

Memories...America...the early years...THANKSGIVING...the fruit... the land...it's singers...politics... Presidents...wars...peace... people...heroes...

WILD NOVEMBER COMES AT LAST!

SEASONS COME AND GO

AND GO AND COME
TO TEACH MEN GRADITUDE

ROBERT POLLACK

—SEASONS COME AND GO—

BACKGROUND: Black paper or fabric.

LETTERS: Large—cut from patterned fabric or wallpaper. Small—white plastic.

METHOD: Trees are made with paper strips and have confetti-like leaf arrangements: 1) white dabs of cotton on a black trunk; 2) light green on brown; 3) dark green on brown; and 4) yellow and orange on tan.

−AMERICA−

BACKGROUND: Light blue paper or fabric.

LETTERS: Large−navy blue cut-out. Small−red.

METHOD: Assemble a collage of old prints. Frame some of these. Use flags, real wheat, political buttons, and documents that are pertinent to American life.

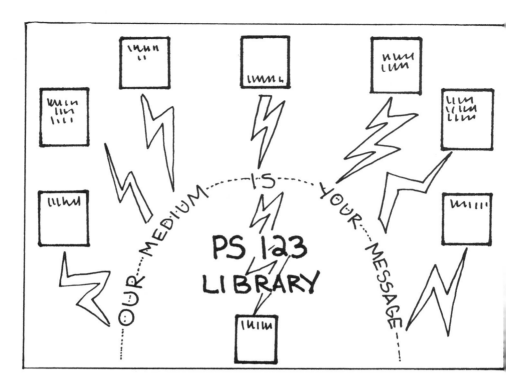

−OUR MEDIUM IS YOUR MESSAGE−

BACKGROUND: Black construction paper or fabric.

LETTERS: Large−white cut-outs. Small−white plastic.

METHOD: Tack large letters over an arc of silver braid or rickrack. Cut electrical signals from posterboard, and cover with aluminum foil. Use book jackets in this display.

ON THE WAY UP   READING GETS EASIER   AND THE REWARDS GET BETTER

−ON THE WAY UP−

BACKGROUND: Black paper or fabric.

LETTERS: Light gray cut-outs.

METHOD: Use charcoal gray posterboard for skyscrapers. Windows are cut from bright yellow construction paper. Apply glue to each window and sprinkle with blue glitter.

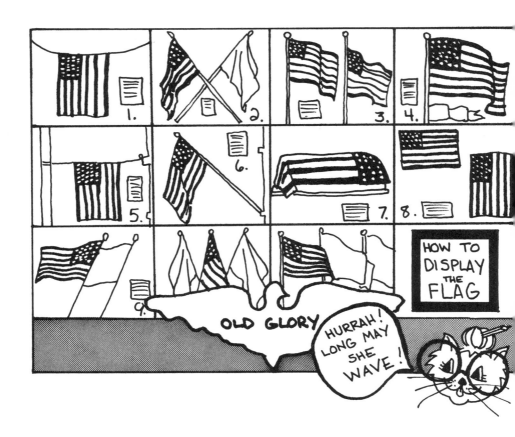

—OLD GLORY—

BACKGROUND: White paper or fabric.

LETTERS: White plastic.

METHOD: Mark off squares with navy soutache braid or narrow grosgrain ribbon. Purchase paper or cloth flags to desired scale. Cut an eagle from gold paper. See an encyclopedia for the proper manner in which to display a flag and for the text of the flag code.

−FOUR FREEDOMS−

BACKGROUND: Black paper or fabric.

LETTERS: Large−black cut-out. Small−black plastic.

METHOD: Use prints of Norman Rockwell's *Four Freedoms*.[1] Mount on red, white, and blue posterboard; laminate for future use. Encircle a Seal of the United States in a round blue paper frame.

---

[1] Obtainable from *The Saturday Evening Post*.

—HEY TURKEY!—

BACKGROUND: Tan burlap.

LETTERS: Large—red cut-out. Small—black marker.

METHOD: Tack real cornstalks, if possible, on both sides of the board. Construct a turkey of brightly colored construction paper. Use strips of red felt on the head and throat. Build a fence with strips of yellow posterboard, and attach a light green posterboard sign.

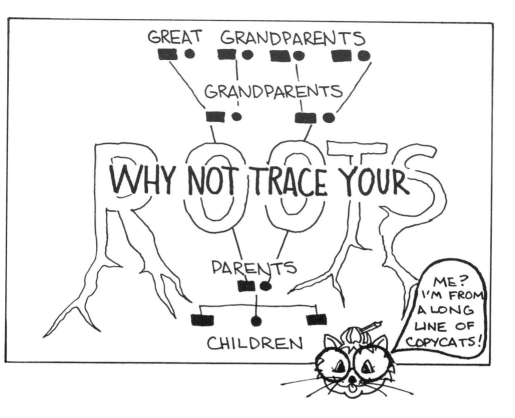

—TRACE YOUR FAMILY TREE—

BACKGROUND: Tan paper or fabric.

LETTERS: Extra-large (ROOTS)—brown cut-out. Large—black cut-out. Small—black plastic.

METHOD: Cut squares and circles from black posterboard. Use black yarn for lines.

—FAR IS VERY NEAR THIS YEAR—

BACKGROUND: White paper or fabric.

LETTERS: Large—black cut-out. Small—black plastic.

METHOD: Framing lines that bracket titles are done with black yarn. Use an opaque projector to enlarge a world map in red. Place small flags on selected countries or, if space permits, use symbols, i.e., U.S.—eagle; Russia—Kremlin.

The way it was

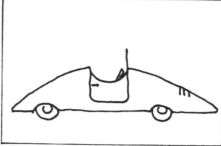

is the way it is

THE CLASSICS ENDURE

—THE WAY IT WAS—

BACKGROUND: Tan paper or fabric.

LETTERS: Large—black cut-out, old-fashioned and modern. Small—black plastic.

METHOD: Use drawings, posters, or available pictures of old/modern cars, airplanes, lovers, or mother and child. Laminate, if possible, and mount to the board.

—FAMILIAR FACES—

BACKGROUND: None necessary.

LETTERS: Large—cut-out, in color complimentary to frames. Small—black plastic.

METHOD: To frame pictures of famous authors or personalities in a plaid or provincial print fabric, cover a mat that has been cut to the necessary size with fabric or wallpaper. See *Southern Living* (August 1980, page 60) for instructions.

—WRITER FOR ALL SEASONS—

BACKGROUND: Each section is two-tone: 1) light/dark blue; 2) tan/brown; 3) white/off-white; and 4) light/dark green. Place the darker color at the bottom.

LETTERS: Large—black cut-out. Small—black plastic.

METHOD: For 1) above, use sparkle string for rays from yellow sun and varicolored blue yarn for water; for 2), make leaves of yellow and orange (imitation leaves can be purchased from a florist); for 3), glue dabs of cotton to resemble snow; for 4), cut green paper leaves and a brown trunk. Tack imitation cherries in the foliage; fringe green paper for grass. Frame a selected writer's portrait and display it with his or her books.

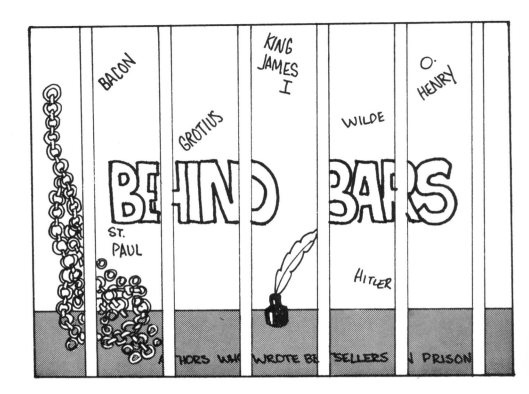

—BEHIND BARS—

BACKGROUND: Tan paper or burlap.

LETTERS: Large—brown cut-out. Small—black plastic.

METHOD: Cut bars from gray posterboard. Make a long paper chain to place behind the bars. See Wallechinsky & Wallace, *Book of Lists* (Morrow, 1975), for a list of authors who wrote in prison.

—FOR THE LIFE OF HIS TIMES—

BACKGROUND: White paper.

LETTERS: Black plastic.

METHOD: Cut car parts from black construction paper. Write slogans with white chalk. The license plate is made of yellow posterboard. Draw in figures with colored markers.

—FARAWAY FACES—

BACKGROUND: None necessary.

LETTERS: Large—black cut-out. Small—black plastic.

METHOD: Use pictures of faces only — man and animal. Wrap the pictures around posterboard squares, taping in back. Align in tight formation.

—THE PRESIDENCY—

BACKGROUND: White paper or fabric.

LETTERS: Large—black cut-out. Small—black plastic.

METHOD: Fashion three strips of crepe paper streamers—red, white, and blue—into the number four. Mount pictures of candidates on light blue posterboard using a dry mount press. Type an abbreviated platform for each candidate, and mount it on light blue posterboard.

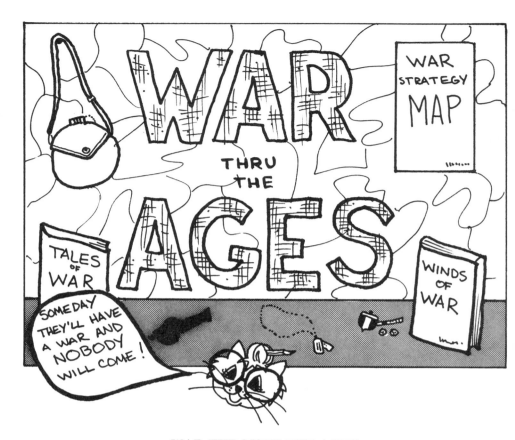

—WAR THROUGH THE AGES—

BACKGROUND: With green, black, and brown construction paper simulate a camouflage effect, or purchase a camouflage-patterned fabric.

LETTERS: Cut from interfaced burlap.

METHOD: Use real or toy items, such as a canteen and a helmet. Your ROTC teacher might provide items for you to use.

—WE REMEMBER THEM—

BACKGROUND: Green paper or fabric. Imitation grass, purchased in rolls, is effective.

LETTERS: Black cut-out.

METHOD: Identical crosses are cut from white posterboard.

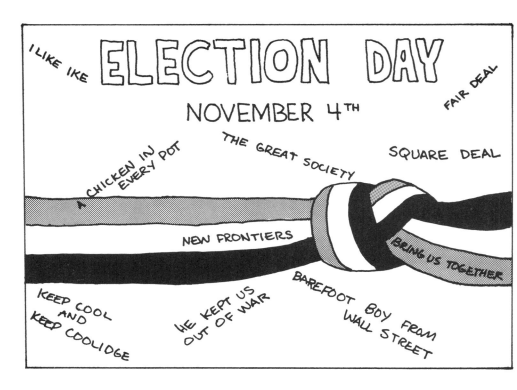

—ELECTION DAY—

BACKGROUND: Light blue paper or fabric.

LETTERS: Large—red cut-out. Slogans in black plastic.

METHOD: Tack wide red, white, and blue fabric strips to the board. Tie the fabric in a knot just off center. Some slogans are:

I Like Ike	A Chicken in Every Pot
New Frontiers	Fair Deal
Square Deal	Back to Normalcy
A Full Dinner Pail	Barefoot Boy from Wall Street
The Great Society	Keep Cool & Keep Coolidge
Bring Us Together	He Kept Us Out of War

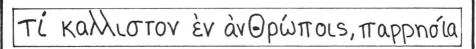

Τί κάλλιστον ἐν ἀνΘρώποις, παρρησία

DIOGENES – APOTHEGM   350 BC.

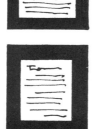

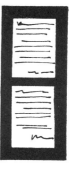

THE MOST BEAUTIFUL THING IN THE WORLD IS FREEDOM OF SPEECH

–FREEDOM OF SPEECH–

BACKGROUND: Old newspaper.

LETTERS: Greek letters are done with black marker on yellow posterboard. Small letters are in black plastic.

METHOD: Mount on black posterboard partial texts of famous speeches on courage or a collection of students' letters to the editor.

DECEMBER:

ANTICIPA-A-TION...

Celebrations...entertainment...
togetherness...charity...children...
brotherhood...Christchild...gifts...
cards...good cheer...candy...12
DAYS OF CHRISTMAS...holly...
carols...star...mistletoe...joy...
Santa Claus...lights...HANUKKAH...
faith...hope...love...

LET THERE BE PEACE...

−LI'L ANGELS−

BACKGROUND: White posterboard.

LETTERS: Red cut-out. Print numbers with black marker.

METHOD: Place a picture of a boy and/or girl in the center of the board. Give each figure a halo of Christmas sparkle string. Also wind sparkle around wings made from coat hangers.

—SANTA CLAUS ON THE ROOF—

BACKGROUND: Black paper.

LETTERS: None.

METHOD: Construct a rooftop with gray posterboard strips. A chimney can be made with brick-patterned crepe paper or red posterboard (marking bricks with black marker). A few paperbacks should be arranged in the top of a burlap bag. Felt mittens should be hung from the chimney. Stars and a moon can be made of paper or stitched in felt (stuff for a three-dimensional effect). Tack cotton batting over rooftop for a final touch.

—WAITING FOR SANTA—

BACKGROUND: Blue paper.

LETTERS: None.

METHOD: Famous animal characters, such as Bugs Bunny or Snoopy, can be substituted for Copycat here. Construct a house from white posterboard. Draw lines with a black marker. Set the house on a bed of cotton batting. Stuff a large Christmas stocking for a body, or cut one from red and green construction paper. A red pom-pom is attached.

—CHIPMUNK CHRISTMAS—

BACKGROUND: White paper.

LETTERS: None.

METHOD: Make earth cross-sections from brown construction paper, tearing it to achieve a rough edge. Cut several layers of green tissue paper strips for grass above ground. Make or purchase an expandable honeycombed tree. Small presents can be purchased at a florist shop. Chipmunks are drawn on brown paper and marked with a black marker.

—DECK THE HALLS—

BACKGROUND: Dark green paper or fabric.

LETTERS: White cut-out.

METHOD: Make or purchase green tissue paper rope. Dot the rope with red berries. Attach purchased elves. Draw a ladder with a black marker, or construct it with posterboard strips if you use a fabric background.

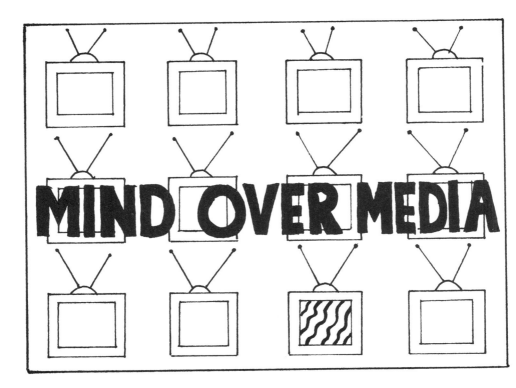

–MIND OVER MEDIA–

BACKGROUND: Yellow paper or fabric.

LETTERS: Black cut-out.

METHOD: Shape squares from dark brown construction paper; edge with a black marker. Glue in the center of each square another square of light gray posterboard covered with acetate. Antennae are made with strong wire covered with aluminum foil (cut into strips and wound around the wire). Display with books on television. Use this board also to feature a special season of the year by placing appropriate pictures on the television screens.

—DOVE OF PEACE—

BACKGROUND: Red paper or fabric.

LETTERS: White shiny paper cut-outs in graduating sizes.

METHOD: Cover posterboard dove with white satin (stuff slightly). Sprinkle the dove with white glitter, or glue white sequins to the bird. Tack the words — Joy, Peace, Love, and Noel — along flightlines of silver soutache braid.

—JOY—

BACKGROUND: Pink or red foil. (It is not necessary to cover the entire board with foil—only the areas visible when the letters are applied.)

LETTERS: Green foil or shiny white paper.

METHOD: Work in thirds, cutting one letter at a time. Place the letters to give the appearance of one piece.

—CHRISTMAS CANDLE—

BACKGROUND: Black fabric.

LETTERS: White plastic.

METHOD: Cut a flame from red foil, and edge it with red and gold Christmas sparkle. The candle is made with green velveteen scrap fabric, taped over a posterboard base. The wick size is determined by the size of your flame: small—pipe cleaner; large—lantern wick.

—AWAY IN A MANGER—

BACKGROUND: Black fabric.

LETTERS: Lower-cased, white plastic.

METHOD: Cover a long, narrow box with brown paper or burlap. Staple the box low on the bulletin board and partially fill it with crumpled newspaper. Use real straw in the remaining space, allowing it to spill over the sides of the box. Wrap a doll in an old baby blanket. Hang or tack oversized star, covered with Christmas sparkle trim. Display alone or with Christmas books.

GIFTS FROM HISTORY AND LITERATURE

TROJAN HORSE

A WATCH AND A COMB

A VISIT FROM ST. NICHOLAS

A STRING OF PEARLS

GOLD, FRANKINCENSE AND MYRRH

LOVE SONNETS

CLEMENT C. MOORE

ELIZABETH BARRETT BROWNING

O. HENRY

GREEK MYTHOLOGY

DE MAUPASSANT

THE BIBLE

Can you match the GIFT with the SOURCE?

—GIFTS FROM HISTORY AND LITERATURE—

BACKGROUND: Red paper or fabric.

LETTERS: Large—white cut-out. Small—white plastic.

METHOD: Construct a tree from molded chickenwire. Tuck squares of green tissue paper into each opening and top with a sparkling star. Place cotton batting around the base of the tree. If possible, place some gifts in opened Christmas boxes, and display with titles such as *Sonnets from the Portuguese*, *The Gift Outright*, *A Visit from St. Nicholas*, and others. The arrangement for Copycat's matching game is as follows:

Trojan Horse   Clement C. Moore
Watch and a Comb   Elizabeth Barrett Browning
Visit from St. Nick   O. Henry
String of Pearls   Greek Mythology
Gold, Frankincense & Myrrh Guy de Maupassant
Love Sonnets   The Bible

−HOLIDAY CUT-UPS−

BACKGROUND: None.

LETTERS: Large−red posterboard. Small−black plastic.

METHOD: Cut varicolored construction paper into appropriate-sized squares. Draw cutting lines and simple sketch on each square with a black marker. Staple red letters over a line of Christmas sparkle string. Ideas for gifts are:

Good for One Car Wash	Two Hours of Walking the Dog
Typing One Term Paper	One Date with Me
Three Kisses	Please Present for One Home-Cooked Meal
One Haircut	
One Shoeshine	Two Hours of Yard Work
	Good for One Birthday Party

—CHRISTMAS CLASSICS—

BACKGROUND: White shiny paper.

LETTERS: Large—red cut-out. Small—green cut-out.

METHOD: Give each box an unusual wrapping. Use rich and shiny paper and ribbon; tie big bows. For added sparkle, staple Christmas garland over each large red letter.

—HAPPY HOLIDAYS—

BACKGROUND: Black fabric.

LETTERS: Write in white yarn or white Christmas decorative trim.

METHOD: Cut mime faces from white posterboard. Paint mouths with bright red lipstick; draw eyes with a black marker. Fashion red and white striped T-shirts from paper, or use purchased French sailor shirts.

—CAROLERS—

BACKGROUND: Top two-thirds—gray paper. Lower third—light blue paper.

LETTERS: None.

METHOD: Figures are assembled from varicolored construction paper. Enlarge carolers using an opaque projector, or employ the graph method. Glue bits of cotton snow over the board.

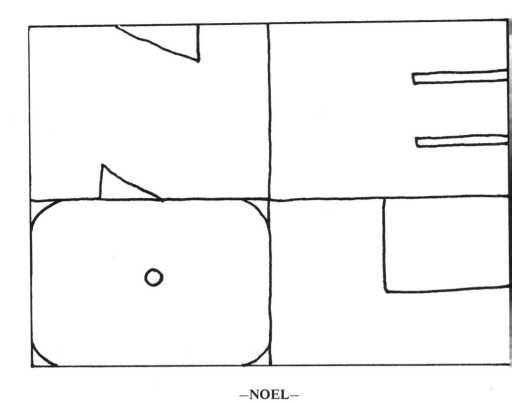

–NOEL–

BACKGROUND: White paper.

LETTERS: Varicolored cellophane (easily obtainable at Eastertime).

METHOD: Make each letter a different color (red, green, pink, and purple). Build lines with gray clay to simulate lead. With a sharp razorblade, carefully cut away openings in letter formations, revealing the white paper beneath.

—HOLIDAYS—

BACKGROUND: Red foil.

LETTERS: Cut-out from silver paper.

METHOD: Draw the outline of a partridge, then staple silver soutache braid along the lines. Silver leaves may be purchased or cut from silver paper. If possible, display books on a bed of more silver leaves, adding three to five silver pears. These, too, can be made or purchased.

—HANUKKAH—

BACKGROUND: White paper.

LETTERS: Red cut-out.

METHOD: Roll on olive green paint. When dry, roll on transparent ink in red and orange to achieve a stone-like quality. Sketch mortar lines with a black marker. Wind red Christmas sparkle string (to simulate a fire) around the form of the Israeli paratrooper insignia that has been fashioned with strong wire.

−DECLARATION OF HUMAN RIGHTS−

BACKGROUND: Light blue fabric.

LETTERS: None.

METHOD: A copy of the Declaration can be obtained from United Nations publications. Cut leaves from white construction paper. Display books and various symbols of oppression, such as barbed wire, chains, handcuffs, and the Star of David.

—PEACE ON EARTH—

BACKGROUND: Light blue paper.

LETTERS: Bright blue paper cut-out.

METHOD: Tack pictures of a variety of animals on the board. Create a jungle by cutting background shrubbery from varitoned green construction paper. Mass clumps of green Easter grass around the bodies.

JANUARY:

RESOLUTIONS...

Bells across the snow...ring out the
old, the false...make a new plan...
ring in the new, the true...hold
standards high...I resolve...
sacrifice and struggle...re-group...
press on...endure...reach out...
grab the brass ring...look up...
catch a falling star... I'M WORTH IT...
touch someone and show I
care...

THIS YEAR REDEEM THE TIME...

–KICK-OFF–

BACKGROUND: Upper board—semicircle of light blue paper. Center board—tan construction paper. Lower board—green grass paper matting (obtainable at most craft shops).

LETTERS: Large—black cut-out. Small—black plastic.

METHOD: Goal posts—white posterboard. Football—brown construction paper with lacing and outline drawn with black marker. Draw in a crowd with a marker. Use bright colored flags along the top of the stadium.

—HIS TRUTH IS MARCHING ON—

BACKGROUND: Black paper or fabric.

LETTERS: Large—white cut-out. Small—white plastic.

METHOD: Cover a shallow square box (bottom and top removed) with white plastic to simulate a pulpit. Hang purple tassled rope in a swag effect. Wrap a posterboard cross with white sparkle garland. Toss a black academic gown over the side of the pulpit and mortarboard nearby. Display with framed pictures relevant to Martin Luther King's life.

—INSTANT NOSTALGIA—

BACKGROUND: White paper.

LETTERS: Black or gold cut-out.

METHOD: Encircle a picture of a lion's head with red wired ribbon, obtainable in many craft shops for under $1.00/yard. Add a felt beret and a paper megaphone. This board will call attention to your audiovisual collection or special film showings in the library.

—SILENT BEAUTY OF WINTER—

BACKGROUND: Light blue paper or fabric.

LETTERS: Write the first three words in blue sparkle string; do "of" in white plastic. Cut the word "Winter" from white flocked paper, fur, or brocade fabric.

METHOD: Frame winter scenes in borderless plexiglass frames. Use Currier & Ives prints or photographs. Display books on mirrors that have been placed on cotton batting on floor of display case.

THOUGHTS FOR THE NEW YEAR

—IF—

BACKGROUND: White paper.

LETTERS: Large—silver (cut with pinking shears). Small—black plastic.

METHOD: Purchase or make white tissue honeycombed bells. Spray with silver paint, and attach a white bow. Type and mount poems[1] on black paper. Remount on silver paper that has been cut with pinking shears.

---

[1] Bible—Matt. 6: 19-34.

Bitterman, Herbert—*Admonition*

Carlyle, Thomas—*To-day*

Frost, Robert—*Road Not Taken*

Houseman, A.E.—*One & Twenty*

Kipling, Rudyard—*If*

Lindsay, Vachel—*The Leaden-eyed*

Teasdale, Sara—*Barter*

Wordsworth, William—*The Rainbow*

Wordsworth, William—*The World Is Too Much with Us*

—SOFTEN THE SNOWS OF WINTER—

BACKGROUND: White paper.

LETTERS: Large—white cut-out, edged with blue marker.

METHOD: Cover the lower area with cotton batting and tuck book jackets here and there. In a window display, fill the floor with white Styrofoam packing nuggets, and bury new books in the simulated snow. Glue dabs of cotton on the board or window to create the appearance of an ongoing blizzard.

—IF WINTER WINDS—

BACKGROUND: Blue paper or fabric.

LETTERS: Large—yellow cut-out. Small—black plastic.

METHOD: Assemble a windmill in segments, enlarging it, if necessary, with an opaque projector. Base and top—black construction paper. Body—tan paper. Make the ladder, railing, and flag staffs with colored yarn. First, determine lines by inserting straight pins at strategic points, then wind yarn once around each pin, pulling the string taut. Tack rectangles of red, yellow, green, and blue scrap fabric for blades. Display with books on humor.

—LOOKING AHEAD—

BACKGROUND: None necessary. However, the stone wall described in the *Hanukkah* board (page 100) would be effective.

LETTERS: Print with black marker; type the poem *The Past* by Ralph Waldo Emerson.

METHOD: Enlarge a profile of Janus, or vary the idea by using pictures of a girl and a boy placed back to back. Mount Janus on imperfect circles (sand on black).

—HOW SAFE IS YOUR HOME?—

BACKGROUND: Light blue paper.

LETTERS: Black plastic.

METHOD: First, determine the positions of the eyes, nose, and mouth. Cover these areas with white paper. Form a cloud with angel hair or white cotton, then lightly spray with black paint. When dry, position openings for the eyes, nose, and mouth (over white areas) by tacking back the material with straight pins. Make a roof-top of gray posterboard strips. Make a red posterboard chimney, and edge bricklines with a black marker. Display with books and rules on safety.

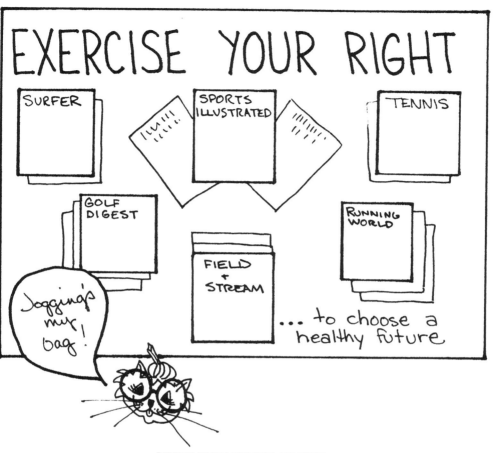

—EXERCISE YOUR RIGHT—

BACKGROUND: None necessary.

LETTERS: Large—black cut-out. Small—black plastic.

METHOD: Tack copies of sports magazines (available in your library) to the board. Offset magazines with covers of previous issues. Display sporting equipment with books if space permits.

−ONCE EACH YEAR−

BACKGROUND: Interesting fabric or wallpaper.

LETTERS: Large−black cut-out. Small−black plastic.

METHOD: Using a black marker, print the sign on white posterboard, making certain that letters diminish in size from top to bottom. Mount the sign on black posterboard, and display with health books.

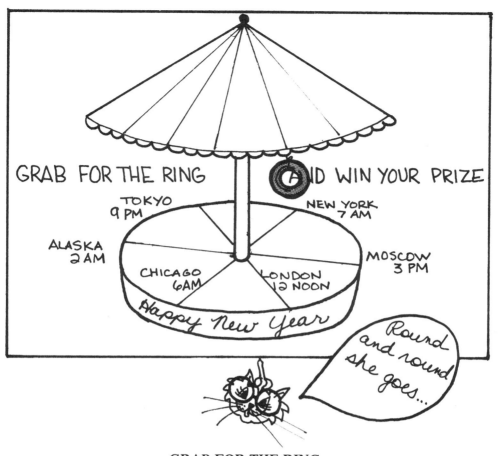

—GRAB FOR THE RING—

BACKGROUND: Bright fabric, i.e., red on yellow polka dot.

LETTERS: Black plastic and black marker.

METHOD: Make a red posterboard canopy, tacked to give a three-dimensional effect. Cut the post and wheel from gray posterboard. Mark with a black marker. Ribbon streamers and large brass ring should fall freely from the canopy.

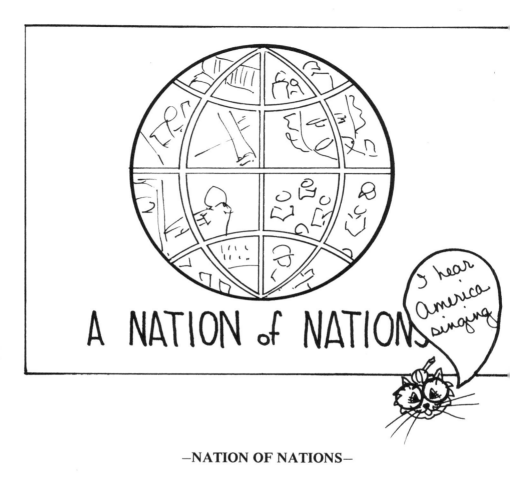

—NATION OF NATIONS—

BACKGROUND: White paper.

LETTERS: Black cut-out.

METHOD: Determine the size of the circle you need. (A pin, chalk, and string make an adequate compass.) Cut a circle from posterboard. Mark separation lines (as shown) and cut. Cover each section with appropriate pictures that have been taken from magazines. Try to use one large picture to cover two adjacent segments — eight pictures in all. Display with books on ethnic literature in America.

—AT HOME—

BACKGROUND: None.

LETTERS: Large—black cut-out. Small—black plastic.

METHOD: Hang a grouping of art works that are for loan to the public as a service of your library. Make use of an easel, if possible. Adapt this arrangement to promote a display of great art books if free loan is not available.

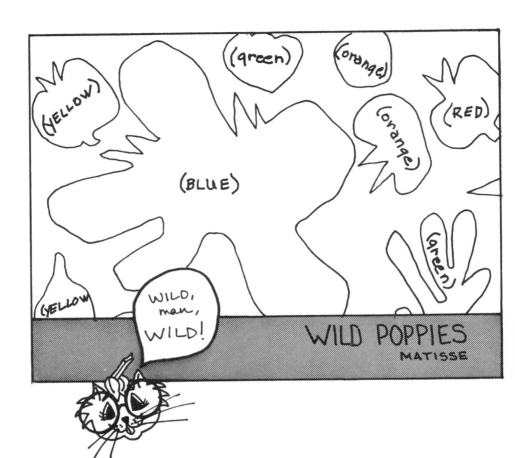

—WILD POPPIES—

BACKGROUND: White paper.

LETTERS: Small—black plastic.

METHOD: Imitate a Matisse painting with water color paints. Colors are indicated in parentheses. Display with art books.

—THE AMERICAN DREAM—

BACKGROUND: White paper.

LETTERS: Large—black cut-out. Small—black pastic.

METHOD: Paint a rainbow with red, yellow, and blue watercolors. Match fragments of shredded paper with appropriate strip of color. Lightly spray cotton clouds with black paint. Display with books on current problems in the United States.

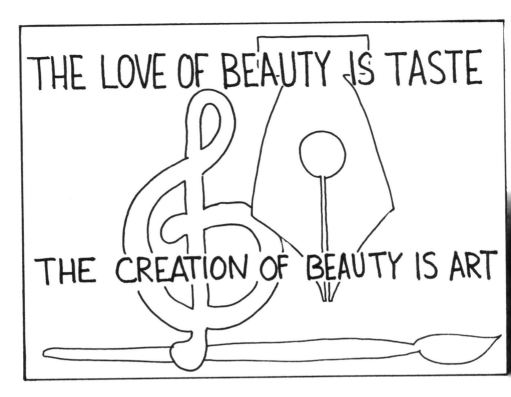

—THE LOVE OF BEAUTY IS TASTE—

BACKGROUND: White paper. Border in blue using felt marker or blue water color paint.

LETTERS: Black cut-out.

METHOD: Enlarge clef, pen point, and brush to desired size on orange, green, and pink construction paper.

—BEAUTY IS IN THE EYE OF THE BEHOLDER—

BACKGROUND: White paper or fabric.

LETTERS: Large—gold on blue cut-out. Small—black plastic.

METHOD: Collect from magazines representative pictures of the various schools of art. Frame the pictures in plexiglass frames, or mount on gold-on-blue paper or posterboard. Cut out faces of gorillas from animal posters; place them cheek to cheek.

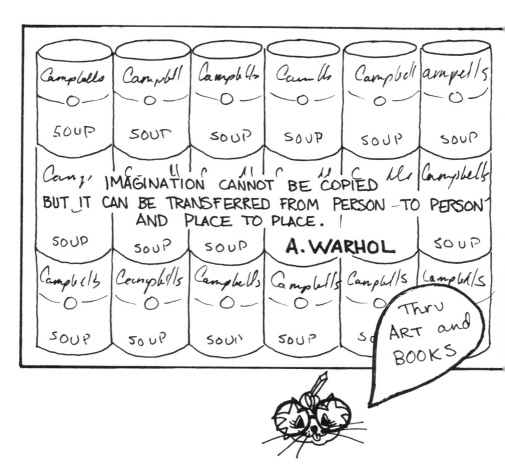

—IMAGINATION CANNOT BE COPIED—

BACKGROUND: Use anything commonplace to make a repetition (such as can labels, pictures, or cereal box fronts).

LETTERS: White plastic.

METHOD: Cover the center area of the board with black construction paper. Spell out the quotation (as shown) on this background.

If I can stop one heart from breaking,
I shall not live in vain;
If I can ease one life the aching,
Or cool one pain,
Or help one fainting robin
Unto his nest again,
I shall not live in vain.

EMILY DICKINSON (1830 - 1886)

—IF I CAN STOP—

BACKGROUND: None.

LETTERS: Cut letters from interfaced cotton print or wallpaper samples. Store these letters in labeled envelopes—one line per package—for future use.

METHOD: Tack to the board (above the poem) Raggedy Ann and Andy dolls, a teddy bear, or any appropriate symbol of childhood love.

FEBRUARY:

THE FUTURE IS NOW...

MID-WINTERTIME...the short month...ice and snow....stir crazy days...get away from it all...hobbies...basketball...goin' steady...hooray for LOVE...the long, hard pull...halfway there...still time to find answers ...time to survive...sunny days are coming...

DANCE INTO SPRING!

—SPACE JOURNEY—

BACKGROUND: Black paper.

LETTERS: Green cut-out, in ever-increasing size (as shown). Spray letters with glue, and sprinkle with blue or green glitter.

METHOD: Cut from construction paper a lime space ship with orange windows. Sketch lines for the control area with a black marker. Purchase a man from outer space, or make one with pipe cleaners and wooden beads.

—S IS FOR SPACE—

BACKGROUND: Black paper or fabric.

LETTERS: Title—silver paper. Names-black plastic.

METHOD: Pin the names of science fiction authors over a blue or silver line of sparkle string. This board is adaptable to numerous subject fields.

—WRITER OF WINTER—

BACKGROUND: Country print—wallpaper or fabric.

LETTERS: Large—white cut-out. Small—white plastic.

METHOD: Make an envelope from four sections of white construction paper. Outline each section with a black marker. Select appropriate stationery; compose representative letters on typewriter and in longhand. Mount the letters on black posterboard, and label them with a white marker.

Put a little **Library** in your **Life**

YOUR AT

FOR SKILLS BUILD

—BUILD SKILLS FOR LIFE—

BACKGROUND: Yellow paper.

LETTERS: White plastic and white yarn for script. Cut from colored paper letters and half-letters for the tops of blocks.

METHOD: Using identical shiny white square boxes (a good person to contact for these is a new bride), attach pictures of young people at work or play to the bottom and top of each box, making a collage (if necessary) to cover the area. Place a letter of the alphabet on each side. A coat of Mod Podge will give an appealing finish to the blocks and will preserve them for future use. Tack the open-ended boxes to the board with the aid of masking tape, placing the tops at the sides and toward the back for a feeling of depth.

—LOVE THY NEIGHBOR—

BACKGROUND: Yellow paper.

LETTERS: Black cut-out.

METHOD: Consult a papercraft manual for instructions on making a red paper sunburst. Use an opaque projector to make patterns for figures: bodies, heads, and guitars. Skirts can be made flat with colored construction paper or, for a three-dimensional effect, can be made in combination with honeycombed tissue semicircles. (See Newman, Thelma. *Paper as Art and Craft*, page 80, for sunburst and page 260 for honeycomb.)

—WHO'S OK? WHO'S NOT OK?—

BACKGROUND: White paper.

LETTERS: White plastic.

METHOD: Use a variety of bright tempera paints and create your own Rorschach test on squares of white paper. Tape these squares over the white background. Consult costume handicraft books for instructions on how to make a clown hat and butterfly. Cut a collar from white posterboard, and attach a gaudy necktie. Display with psychology books.

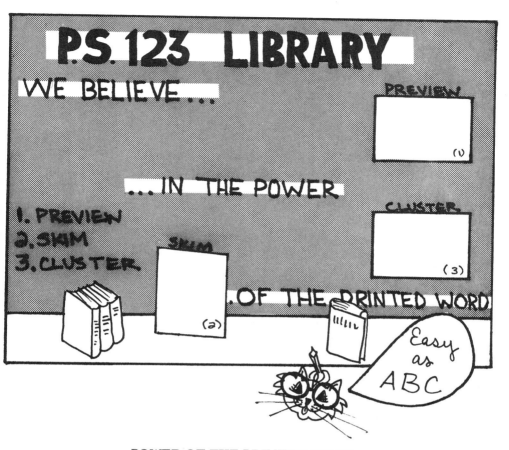

—POWER OF THE PRINTED WORD—

BACKGROUND: Newsprint.

LETTERS: Black cut-out. Numbers with words are color-keyed to examples set forth on the board: 1) orange, 2) purple, and 3) green. Make two copies of each word.

METHOD: For easy viewing, tack black letters over white posterboard slats. Mount an example of each rule (obtained from old texts and magazines) on paper color-keyed to a number, and mark as follows: 1) PREVIEW (texts)—Using an orange marker, bracket first and last paragraphs, and underline the first sentence of intervening paragraphs; 2) SKIM (adventure)—Circle key words in purple; 3) CLUSTER (to increase speed and comprehension)— Circle three or four word groupings in green. Staple second set of letters across the top of each mounting.

—HARLEM RENAISSANCE—

BACKGROUND: Blue paper.

LETTERS: Blue and silver sparkle string.

METHOD: Print or type names of black writers[1] on white cards. Glue one card to each star that has been cut from heavy silver paper. Cut a New York skyline from black paper, marking window lines with chalk.

---

[1]
Arna Bontemps	Charles Johnson	Claude McKay
Countee Cullen	James Weldon Johnson	Jean Toomer
Langston Hughes	Alain Locke	Carl Van Vechten

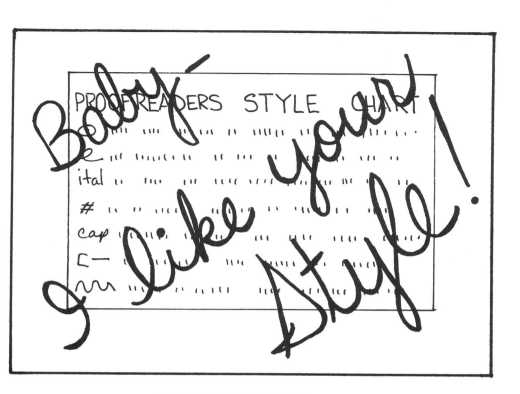

—BABY—I LIKE YOUR STYLE—

BACKGROUND: None necessary.

LETTERS: Script in red elephant yarn.

METHOD: Make your own proofreader's style chart, or purchase a commercially printed poster. Language Arts is a particularly good source for this item.

—LOVE ALWAYS—

BACKGROUND: White paper or valentine print fabric.

LETTERS: White cut-out edged with marker.

METHOD: To a base of red posterboard, attach pictures of film stars, athletes, faculty members, or any persons who have strong youth appeal. Fashion a variety of frames, as ornate as your supplies allow. Try to use gold paper, red and white lace doilies, lace and lots of ribbon. Construct a mailbox from blue posterboard; decorate with pink and red hearts.

—I LOVE YOU—

BACKGROUND: White paper or fabric.

LETTERS: Black marker.

METHOD: Print letters on large red posterboard heart. Circle "I love you" in white marker. Frame the board with simulated frosting of pink elephant yarn. You can use a real cake decorator tube or construct one with gray posterboard, and place it on the board as illustrated.

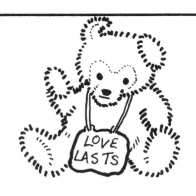

DO YOU LOVE ME
OR DO YOU NOT?
YOU TOLD ME ONCE
BUT I FORGOT.

ANON.

Actions speak louder...

—DO YOU LOVE ME?—

BACKGROUND: None necessary.

LETTERS: Oversized provincial print cut-out.

METHOD: Tack a forlorn-looking teddy bear to the board, and put a sign around his neck.

—SOUND OFF—ONE, TWO—

BACKGROUND: White paper or fabric.

LETTERS: Red cut-out.

METHOD: Cut a horn from gold or blue paper (make a pattern from news-paper first, to avoid error). Edge the mouth of the horn with gold sparkle string, and make sound waves of silver and gold. Red lace doily hearts should frame pictures of famous couples. The couples should run the gamut from the President of the United States and his wife to well-known school sweethearts.

—GAME OF HEARTS—

BACKGROUND: Pink paper.

LETTERS: Large—red yarn script. Small—white plastic.

METHOD: Cover the roof, which has been made with three corrugated angles, with wide-to-narrow strips of dark-to-light green paper; scallop or fringe the lower edges. Staple the strips horizontally to the center triangle, beginning at the base with the widest and darkest strips. Note the change in line in the adjacent angles. Cut columns and latticework from white posterboard. Pin rag dolls to gray steps, arranging playing cards in their hands and about their feet. Place red and pink hearts around the dolls' heads.

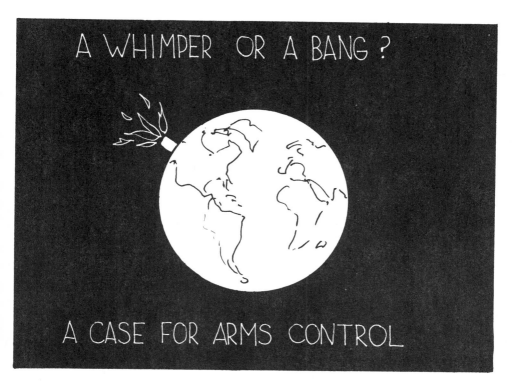

—A WHIMPER OR A BANG?—

BACKGROUND: Black paper or fabric.

LETTERS: Large—white cut-out. Small—white plastic.

METHOD: Mount a picture of the world on a corrugated paper circle. Cut a fuse from gray posterboard, and attach an oversized wick; then add flames of red sparkle string.

—THE COMMON MARKET—

BACKGROUND: Light blue paper.

LETTERS: Dark green cut-out.

METHOD: Enlarge a map of Europe and make countries inside the fence of light green construction paper; those outside, of dark green paper. Attach purchased miniature carriers of goods, i.e., boats, trains, and trucks. Draw a fence in black marker. Stand toy soldiers along the border. Place objects as if they were being viewed from the air.

—WORLD POWER—

BACKGROUND: Black paper or fabric.

LETTERS: Red cut-out.

METHOD: Use white muslin and striped cotton fabric for Arab headdress. Fit the headdress over a picture of a globe (after padding the pate with cotton batting). With the help of handicraft books, make paper editions of hats representing Alexander the Great, the Pope, and Caesar (laurel wreath). Cut a swastika, Charlemagne monogram, and hammer and sickle from red posterboard. Hang each small item on an appropriate book.

—WHAT NEXT IN JERUSALEM?—

BACKGROUND: Dark blue paper or fabric.

LETTERS: Large—light blue cut-out. Small—light blue cut-out and black plastic.

METHOD: Cut a skyline from black construction paper; mark windows and doorways with yellow chalk. Cut a dome from gold paper, and mount on a corrugated board.

—OLYMPIC FLAG—

BACKGROUND: White paper or fabric.

LETTERS: None.

METHOD: Use elephant yarn (available at most hobby shops) to make five rings, each a different color: blue, yellow, black, green, and red. Display the rings with materials and books on the Olympic games or sports in general.

—WILL YOU JOIN THE DANCE?—

BACKGROUND: None.

LETTERS: Large—black cut-out. Small—black plastic.

METHOD: Offset one to three Degas prints with a velveteen curtain and fringed tiebacks. See *Slapdash Decorating* by Carol Barkin and Elizabeth James for ideas for curtain arrangement. Display with books on the dance.

MARCH:

NOW COMES IN THE SWEET OF THE YEAR...

forth issues the bee....and me
...trumpeting news of sunshine
and flowers...daffodils...clouds
and kites...winds that whirl...
signs of life...growth...Lent...
hope on the rise....time to sow
IN LIKE A LION...

OUT LIKE A LAMB!

−THE NEW JOURNALISM−

BACKGROUND: Black paper or fabric.

LETTERS: White cut-out.

METHOD: On squares of white posterboard, stencil a single letter (use a variety of styles and colors). Arrange squares in crossword puzzle form. Superimpose over the letters pictures of authors and/or book titles pertinent to the new journalism, i.e., John Barth, Donald Bartheime, Truman Capote, E. L. Doctorow, Kate Millett, John Updike, Kurt Vonnegut, and Tom Wolfe.

—TOOLS OF THE TRADE—

BACKGROUND: None.

LETTERS: Cut large letters from newsprint, and mount on slightly larger letters cut from black paper.

METHOD: Make pencils from brightly colored construction paper. Draw in lines and pencil points with a black marker. Display with books on writing: style, grammar, usage, and the like.

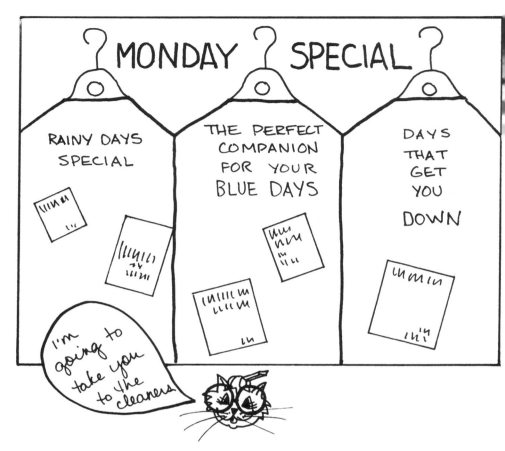

—MONDAY SPECIAL—

BACKGROUND: None.

LETTERS: Large—black cut-out. Small—colored felt pens.

METHOD: Make (or beg from your local cleaner) white garment bags, and suspend from brightly colored plastic hangers. Print various phrases directly on the bags, and tack new book jackets here and there. Vary the appearance of the board by using see-through plastic bags and tacking book covers inside. Cut letters from colorful felt.

−THINK METRIC−

BACKGROUND: Yellow paper.

LETTERS: Large−black cut-out. Small−black plastic.

METHOD: Draw rule lines and numbers with a large black marker before tacking the title. Cover two lightweight boxes—one with graph paper, the other with blue construction paper. Collect 10 paper-made frozen juice cans to represent deciliters. Outline liter shape with red yarn.

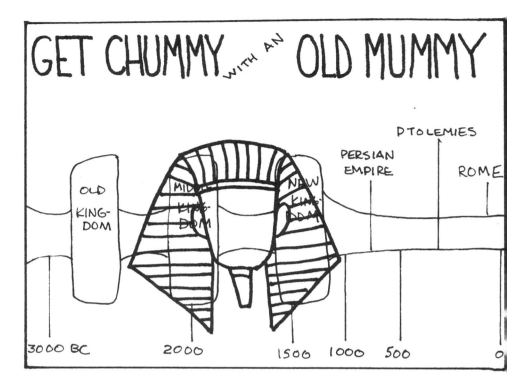

—GET CHUMMY WITH AN OLD MUMMY—

BACKGROUND: None.

LETTERS: Large—light on dark cut-out. Small—black plastic.

METHOD: Cut three rectangles from a suitably figured wallpaper or gift wrap. Connect the rectangles with dark yarn. You can achieve the King Tut outline by strategically placing straight pins and using a gold soutache braid. The pins (hardly visible) serve as anchors as you wind the braid around them to complete the picture. Display with books on archeology and Egyptology.

—TRUMPET OF A PROPHECY—

BACKGROUND: Dark brown paper (telephone poles). Center portion—blue/gray paper.

LETTERS: Dark blue cut-out or black plastic.

METHOD: Sketch pole markings with a black marker. Tack wire from one pole to the other, and attach birds. Use pictures of birds or purchase clip-on birds at a florist shop. Let a few birds appear as if they're flying freely (if possible). Spray the poster all over with simulated snow.

—ALTERNATIVES TO COLLEGE—

BACKGROUND: White paper.

LETTERS: Cut from stencils—any color.

METHOD: During the year, collect hats that are representative of types of work where a college degree is not necessary.[1] Construct a hat rack with black posterboard. Glue small woodblocks behind some hooks, so the hooks will stand away from the board. Hang some hats from the hooks, and tack others (as shown). Hang a dollar sign on mortarboard.

---

[1]
Armed forces hats	Eyeshade	Police hat
Artist's beret	Hard hat	Railroad cap
Baker's hat	Painter's cap	Ski cap
Baseball cap	Miner's hat	

—EVERYTHING IS FUNNY—

BACKGROUND: Newspaper comic section.

LETTERS: Large—black cut-out. Small—black plastic.

METHOD: Mount a picture of an American humorist, such as Will Rogers, on black posterboard. Write graffiti[1] directly on the comics with a black marker. Cover boxes with funnies also, placing a variety of humor books inside.

---

[1] Consult Joseph Littell's *The Comic Spirit*, page 118.

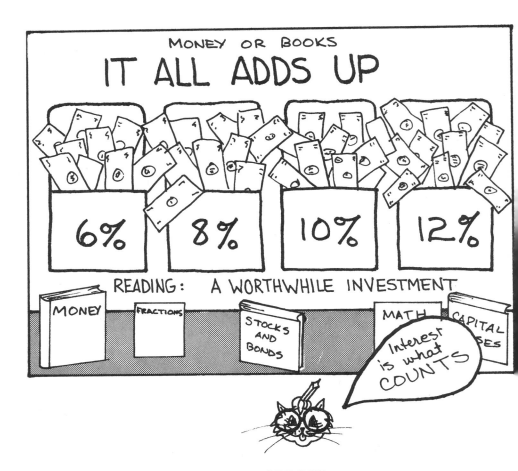

—IT ALL ADDS UP—

BACKGROUND: Pink paper or fabric.

LETTERS: Large—dark green posterboard cut-out. Small—black plastic.

METHOD: Using sand construction paper, fashion four book pockets patterned after a library book pocket. Insert clusters of green play money at the opening of each pocket. Display with math books, ranging from the easy to the difficult.

—WHO REALLY OWNS THE UNITED STATES?—

BACKGROUND: None.

LETTERS: Cross-stitch letters in the sign with a felt pen. Other letters are of black plastic or cut-out.

METHOD: Frame and hang the sign. Attach three hooks to hold the fez, turban, and Arab headdress. Collect labels or advertising of companies that have heavy foreign investments[1] in the United States.

---

[1] Consult *Business Week* (July 9, 1979), page 50.

—PAST IS PROLOGUE—

BACKGROUND: None.

LETTERS: Oversized letters of black posterboard cut-out. Mount on corrugated board for three-dimensional effect.

METHOD: Color is the basis of this board. Tear the smallest mountain from dark red construction paper; the next, is a lighter red. The tallest mountain is made from orange paper. Cover the remaining board with yellow paper. Books of all kinds can be used in this display.

—TO KNOW A COUNTRY AND ITS PEOPLE—

BACKGROUND: Blue or gray paper.

LETTERS: White plastic.

METHOD: The Russian skyline is made with felt markers and green, rust, sand, gray, and shades of orange construction paper. Construct the main turret in three dimensions. Do this by first winding a long strip of paper, then later unwinding it upward on the board, stapling it down as you proceed. Glue windows last.

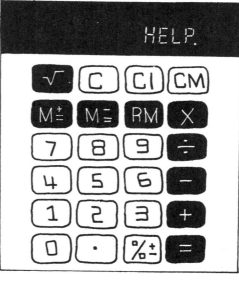

MATH A PROBLEM?

COME TO THE LIBRARY

HELP.

TUTORS AVAILABLE THRU NATIONAL HONOR SOCIETY

—MATH A PROBLEM?—

BACKGROUND: None.

LETTERS: Large—blue cut-out. Small—black plastic.

METHOD: Cut computer buttons from white posterboard. Mark with a black felt pen. (Be sure also to edge in black.) Glue buttons to white posterboard that has been mounted on a black base. "Help" is outlined with red sparkle string.

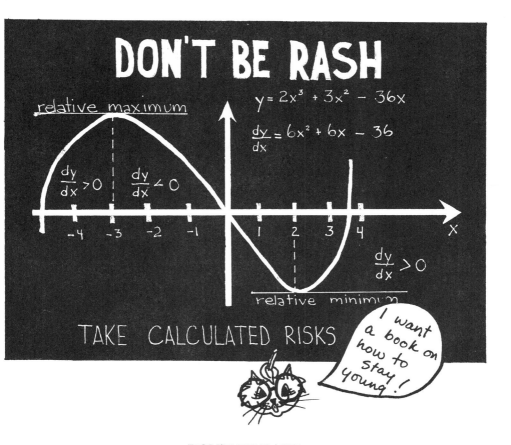

—DON'T BE RASH—

BACKGROUND: Black construction paper.

LETTERS: Large—white cut-out. Small—white plastic.

METHOD: Draw a calculus display in chalk as follows: Graph lines—white; Equation—yellow; Remainder—red or pink. Display with "How to" books in various fields.

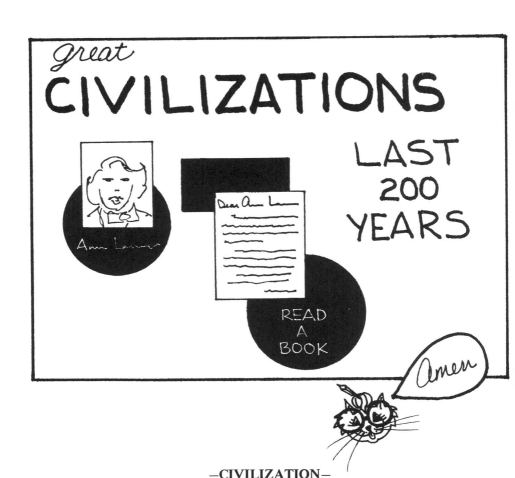

—CIVILIZATION—

BACKGROUND: White shelf paper.

LETTERS: Write the word "Great" and the number 200 in black yarn. Cut large letters from black constrruction paper squares. Use white plastic on black off-sets.

METHOD: Mount a photo of any famous newspaper columnist, and display it with a provocative article. Type the item (primary type preferred), and mount against black off-sets. This board was based on an Ann Landers' column, *Great Civilizations Last 200 Years*. Write the *Chicago Sun-Times* for photo and text.

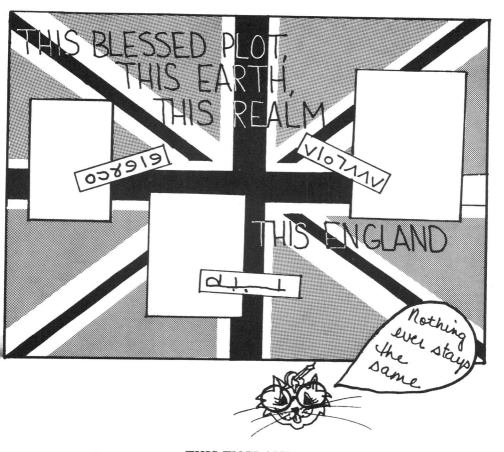

—THIS ENGLAND—

BACKGROUND: White paper.

LETTERS: Black plastic or cut-out.

METHOD: Construct a British flag with bright blue and red construction paper. Observe your model closely; this is a tricky flag to reproduce. Tack travel posters of familiar British landmarks, such as Big Ben, Parliament, Beefeaters, on the board. With a black marker, print signs in Arabic on white posterboard, and place on the buildings.

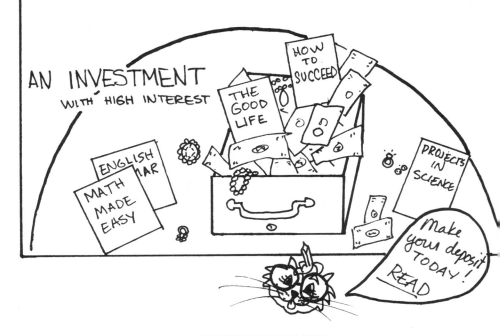

—SAFETY DEPOSIT—

BACKGROUND: Black construction paper.

LETTERS: Large—white cut-out. Small—white plastic.

METHOD: Tack an arc of gold tinsel garland on the board. Construct a safety deposit box with gray and red posterboard. Affix a brass handle. Play money, jewelry, and book covers should be piled inside the open drawer. Post a list of suggested books nearby.

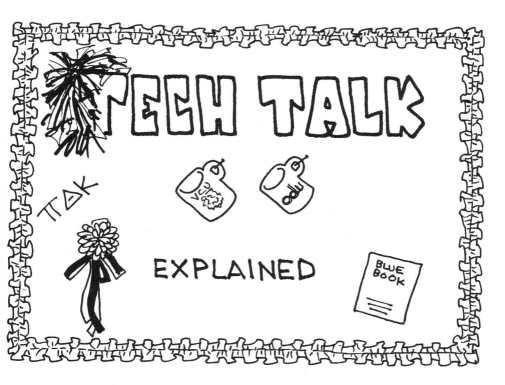

−TECH TALK EXPLAINED−

BACKGROUND: None. You are creating a bulletin board within a bulletin board.

LETTERS: Large−felt cut-outs in school colors. Small−black plastic.

METHOD: Gather crepe paper streamers in the school's colors to border the display. Borrow memorabilia−such as mugs, monograms, T-shirts, and mementos of traditional activities−from someone associated with the college you have selected to feature.

a place for high achievers

P.S. 123 LIBRARY

—PLACE FOR HIGH ACHIEVERS—

BACKGROUND: Light blue paper.

LETTERS: Large—dark green cut-out. Small—black plastic.

METHOD: Copy a tree with strokes of a black marker. (These pens can be purchased in very large sizes in art supply shops.) Make a red kite, fancy or plain, and tie red rags on a black yarn tail.

—YOU DON'T HAVE TO BE IRISH—

BACKGROUND: Green paper or fabric.

LETTERS: Black plastic, or print with a felt pen.

METHOD: Cut two circles from black posterboard. Make hair from black yarn (stitch mother's locks on the sewing machine), and glue to each head. Use real or paper Indian headbands and feathers. Lightly stuff an old blanket with fiberfill, and wrap in a criss-cross fashion with plastic string. Edge white speech clouds with a black or green marker. Display with books about Ireland and the Irish.

APRIL:

THE 1ST OF APRIL SOME DO SAY IS SET APART FOR ALL FOOL'S DAY...

Fickle...jewel of time...age feels youth...NATURE'S JOY... insects...leaves...flowers... showers and sunshine chase each other...casual with miracles ...EASTERTIME...

RESURRECTION

—ONE OF A KIND—

BACKGROUND: Black fabric.

LETTERS: Gold cut-out.

METHOD: Use a variety of gold braid trim, and tack to serve as the border of a heraldic shield. Use a picture of a unicorn or enlarge this comical one on gold paper. Feature classic reference books.

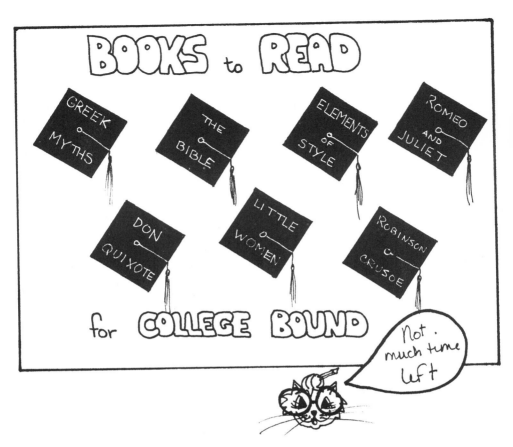

—BOOKS TO READ BEFORE COLLEGE—

BACKGROUND: White paper or fabric.

LETTERS: Large—black cut-out. Small—black plastic.

METHOD: Cut out black posterboard squares. Stencil and cut letters from white construction paper, and glue to simulated mortarboards. Hang varicolored tassles at the center of each square. These can be purchased or made with yarn.

—WE'VE GOT YOU COVERED—

BACKGROUND: Dark gray paper.

LETTERS: Script in yellow yarn. Print—white plastic.

METHOD: Cut an umbrella from black construction paper. Cover posterboard handle with aluminum foil. Glue bits and pieces of foil over the umbrella.

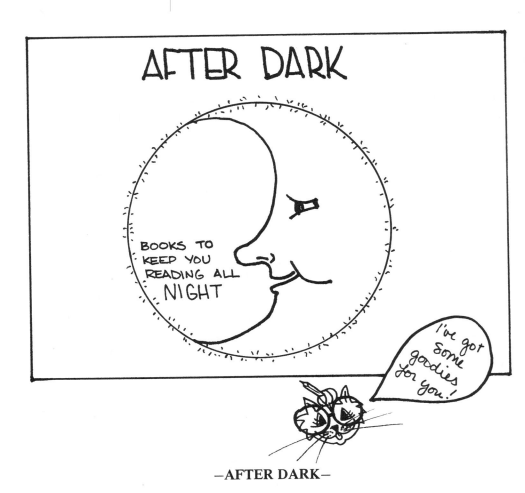

—AFTER DARK—

BACKGROUND: Black paper or fabric.

LETTERS: Gold tinsel garland. Small—black plastic.

METHOD: Cut Mr. Moon from yellow posterboard. Draw his face with a black marker. Staple more tinsel garland around the circle. Display with books on high adventure and mystery.

—SPEAK THE SPEECH—

BACKGROUND: Light blue paper or fabric.

LETTERS: Black cut-out.

METHOD: Cut fragmented semicircles from red posterboard, and varishaped microphones from black posterboard. Use black yarn for wires. Display with books on public speaking, quotations, and/or monologues.

—TO ADMIRE BENEATH YOUR BONNET—

BACKGROUND: Green paper or fabric.

LETTERS: Write in pink yarn.

METHOD: Cut the brim and bonnet from posterboard, and cover both with a provincial print, stuffing the bonnet segment with cotton batting. Attach colored ribbons. Edge inexpensive mirror with lace, and cut handle from white posterboard. Display with books and magazines on beauty care, health foods, exercise, and similar subjects.

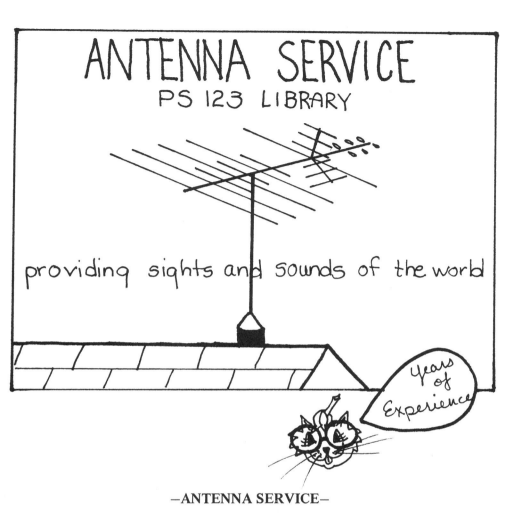

ANTENNA SERVICE
PS 123 LIBRARY

providing sights and sounds of the world

Years of Experience

—ANTENNA SERVICE—

BACKGROUND: Light blue paper or fabric.

LETTERS: Large—dark blue cut-out. Small—black plastic.

METHOD: Cut roof from white posterboard, and sketch lines with black marker. Cover two garden sticks with aluminum foil for antenna "T". Also cover narrow wooden dowels for remaining segments, or sketch with marker, carefully observing line direction and length.

—THE REAL THING—

BACKGROUND: Figured fabric: stripe, check, or polka dot.

LETTERS: Pick up the darkest color in the fabric and use for cut-out lettering. Yarn script.

METHOD: Place books and/or story titles with themes of imitation, fakery, irony, and mistaken identity[1] in painted shadow boxes. Recordings can also be used here to display with the titles you have selected.

---

[1] Cheever, John—*The Duchess*
de Maupassant, Guy—*The Necklace*
Henry, O.—*Gift of the Magi*

Irving, Washington—*Spectre Bridegroom*
James, Henry—*The Real Thing*
Munro, Hector Hugh—*The Hounds of Hate*

—EASTER EGGS—

BACKGROUND: Pink paper, or try plastic Styrofoam egg cartons (covers removed) tacked in tight formation for an interesting background in a large window display. These cartons are available at your grocer's in pastel shades.

LETTERS: Large—white cut-out. Small—white plastic.

METHOD: Cover Styrofoam eggs in rich fabrics, such as brocade, velveteen, and satin. Use opulent trims. Hang the eggs with ribbon, or affix them with florist picks. Let plastic eggs spill out of a basket; nest others in Easter grass. Type labels (100-900), and glue to eggs.

—TURN WINTER INTO SPRING—

BACKGROUND: Light blue paper or fabric.

LETTERS: Large—white cut-out. Small—white plastic.

METHOD: Cut snowflakes in assorted sizes from varicolored pastel tissue paper. Hang the flakes with wire or thread. Make an assortment of paper flowers. Tack some blossoms to the board but give others pipe cleaner stems. Tack large lettering over blue yarn and establish base line with bright green yarn.

—BOOKS ON THE HOUSE—

BACKGROUND: Light blue paper.

LETTERS: Large—dark green cut-out. Small—black plastic.

METHOD: Apply lettering first. Lightly sketch an outline of a house. Go over these lines again with felt markers; using red, black, and brown. For windows, cut rectangles from dark green construction paper, and make slats over the windows in white. Cut shrubbery from green paper in both dark and light shades.

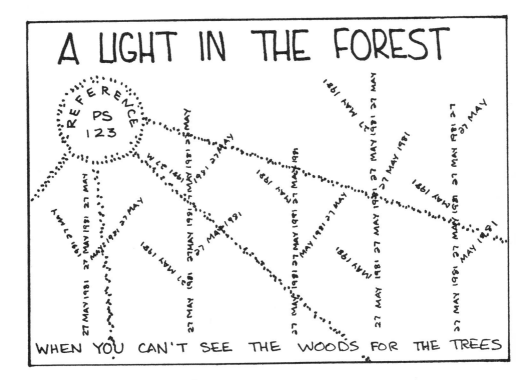

—LIGHT IN THE FOREST—

BACKGROUND: Light green paper.

LETTERS: Large—dark green cut-out. Small—black plastic.

METHOD: Pencil sketch trees.[1] Using a green felt marker, print in close repetition a due date (day, month, and year) along these lines. Cut a stencil for this step, if you prefer. The forest light is a circle of green foil, bordered with the same green sparkle garland used for the emanating rays.

---

[1] This board is based on an idea from *Alphabet and Images* by Maggie Gordon, pages 88-89.

—GOLDEN OPPORTUNITY—

BACKGROUND: Yellow paper or fabric.

LETTERS: Black marker.

METHOD: Alternate strips of dark blue and green posterboard for water, and make a circle of red for the sun. Draw the bridge using a ruler and a felt pen, applying a combination of orange and black yarn over some of the lines for emphasis.

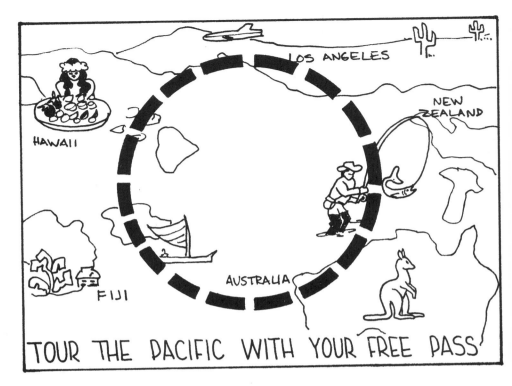

—TOUR THE PACIFIC—

BACKGROUND: Light blue paper or fabric.

LETTERS: Black plastic.

METHOD: Cut out map areas from old maps or colored construction paper. Use a descriptive picture on the large land areas (such as a kangaroo for Australia). Tack a circle, made with black construction paper segments, on the board; this is the focal point, so make it large.

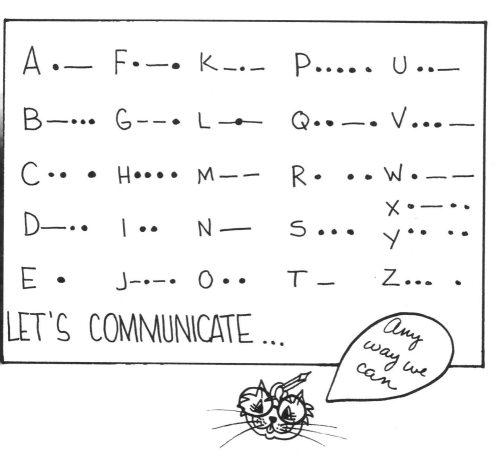

—LET'S COMMUNICATE—

BACKGROUND: White paper.

LETTERS: Alphabet—black cut-out. Slogan—black plastic.

METHOD: Draw dots and dashes with a large-point black marker.

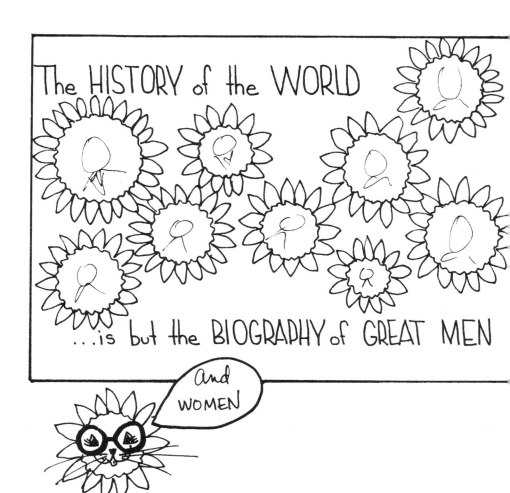

–HISTORY OF THE WORLD–

BACKGROUND: Green paper or imitation grass.

LETTERS: White cut-out.

METHOD: Make a collection of pictures of famous people, and mount the pictures on yellow posterboard circles. Frame each picture with white paper petals, and edge with yellow rickrack.

—NOBODY'S PERFECT—

BACKGROUND: None.

LETTERS: Red cut-out.

METHOD: Cut figures from folded newspaper. Break up the figures with slats of black posterboard. Display with biographies. This board can also be used to feature books on self-improvement or psychology.

—LATE STARTERS—

BACKGROUND: Blue paper.

LETTERS: White plastic.

METHOD: Shoe and lace holes are shaped from white construction paper, with red trim. Wide, dark blue speedlines are offset with narrow lines, ruled with a felt pen.

−SEE 822.3−SHAKESPEARE−

BACKGROUND: Top area−light blue paper. Lower third−green paper or imitation grass.

LETTERS: White cut-out and black marker.

METHOD: Cut dominoes from black and white construction paper. A preliminary sketch will be most helpful in determining lines and placement of the dominoes.

—APRIL FOOLS' DAY—

BACKGROUND: Lime green paper.

LETTERS: Black cut-out.

METHOD: Enlarge a picture of a zebra to size on a sheet of the same green paper used for the background. Mark stripes and facial features with a black marker. After mounting the zebra on the board, attach a black wool fringe for the mane and tail.

MAY:

NOW IS THE MONTH OF MAYING...

Lilac time...the sound of the bird...music everywhere...poetry ...MOTHER'S DAY...laughter and youth...and warm desire... freedom to...gather me rose-buds...

DEWEY IS THE MORNING UPON THE 1ST OF MAY...

—AN OPEN BOOK—

BACKGROUND: Dark green paper.

LETTERS: Black marker. Copycat quote in black plastic.

METHOD: The key, sign, lock, and doorknob are cut from yellow posterboard and marked with a black marker. Affix heavy paper spring to the underside of the doorknob. Use a stuffed animal to hold the key.

—COTTON CANDY—

BACKGROUND: Gray paper.

LETTERS: Large—red cut-out. Small—black plastic.

METHOD: Cotton candy is made wth polyester fiberfill, wound on garden stakes and sprayed with pink paint. Fill the board with raindrops of aluminum foil or silver sequins. Include a picture of poetess, Nikki Giovanni, if available.

—GUYS AND DOLLS—

BACKGROUND: None.

LETTERS: Medium and large—black and brown cut-out. Small—black plastic.

METHOD: Tack black yarn to mark the border of the "Wanted" poster. Four champagne-type corks serve as nails. For emphasis, glue these to black construction paper patches. Place two inexpensive mirrors, as shown. Display with books on guidance and study skills.

—LIBRARIES ARE FOR PEOPLE—

BACKGROUND: Pink paper or fabric.

LETTERS: Black plastic.

METHOD: Tack a border of red elephant yarn, beginning and ending with two "1's" in the slogan. Sketch a desk with a black marker. Cut a librarian from white posterboard. Cut rows of identical figures from folded construction paper, using a different color for each row.

—YOU DON'T SAY—

BACKGROUND: White shelf paper.

LETTERS: None.

METHOD: Do a fingerpainting on an entire white background. Tack signs and buttons that you have collected. Three monkeys that see, hear, and speak no evil (signified either by colored paper mittens, or by tape, a blindfold, and earmuffs) should be placed on the board.

−HIGH BOOK PRICES−

BACKGROUND: Light green paper.

LETTERS: Large−white cut-out, sprinkled with green glitter. Small−black plastic.

METHOD: With a black marker, adapt and reproduce a facsimile of your library permit. Do this directly on the green background or on white posterboard. The dollar sign is made with green tinsel garland.

—UNIQUE TO YOU—

BACKGROUND: None.

LETTERS: Large—black cut-out. Small—black plastic.

METHOD: Cut black construction paper to simulate a filmstrip. Indicate all open areas with white paper. Cut out your state in red silhouette, and mount. This board can have many other uses.

—I REMEMBER MAMA—

BACKGROUND: Light blue paper or fabric.

LETTERS: Pink and blue chalk or cut-outs.

METHOD: Attach a swinging brace high on the board; wind imitation green garland around it. Arrange a doll in a small basket, under bedclothes, and hang the basket with pink and blue ribbon. Print with chalk on white paper cloud, or staple cut-out letters on a puff of cotton.

—EMPTY NEST—

BACKGROUND: Opaque pink gift wrap paper.

LETTERS: Green yarn script and white plastic.

METHOD: Before building the nest of straw, make provisions for hanging the nest by first attaching masking tape tabs to the Styrofoam base. With the aid of florist pins, cover this base with straw, pine, or hay in the same way you would apply greens to a wreath base. Spray with fixative. When dry, glue broken eggshells in the center of the nest. Add the date that has been cut from green construction paper.

—HERE IS WHERE IT'S AT—

BACKGROUND: None.

LETTERS: Black plastic.

METHOD: The sleeve, cuff, and hand are made from posterboard—sleeve and cuff of white (draw checks with red marker); fingers in sand. Tie red yarn around the index finger.

—NOTABLE AMERICAN WOMEN—

BACKGROUND: Light blue paper or fabric.

LETTERS: Red cut-out.

METHOD: Using an opaque projector, enlarge a picture of the crown of the Statue of Liberty on black or dark gray construction paper. Display with books about women. This board can be used for many subjects on American history, i.e., immigrants.

—MOTHER—

BACKGROUND: White paper.

LETTERS: Pink and white checked, interfaced fabric, cut with pinking shears.

METHOD: Display with pictures of mother and child (human or animal), along with books on family life.

—MUSIC IN THE AIR—

BACKGROUND: White paper if staffs are drawn with black marker; none if constructed with black yarn.

LETTERS: Black plastic.

METHOD: Construct music stands in two dimensions out of black posterboard. Feature composers or performers on each stand.

—MUSIC AND ALL THAT JAZZ—

BACKGROUND: Gray paper or fabric.

LETTERS: Large—white cut-out. Small—black plastic.

METHOD: Cut a grand piano from black construction paper. The keyboard is a strip of white posterboard to which black paper keys are glued.

—LIVE THE LEGEND—

BACKGROUND: Black paper or fabric.

LETTERS: Gold cut-out.

METHOD: Silver swords and a shield of royal blue are made with poster-board. Make the gold crown with paper or braid, or a combination of the two. Consult a cardboard handicraft book for instructions on making the knight's helmet. Drape filmy white georgette from a hennin made of posterboard. The swords can be reused on a board of your own design under the caption, *Straight and to the Point*.

−INSIGHT−

BACKGROUND: Green paper.

LETTERS: Black plastic.

METHOD: Sketch the lines of a maze before finally marking them with an extra-wide black marker. The center rectangle contains a collage of pictures of adolescents' faces.

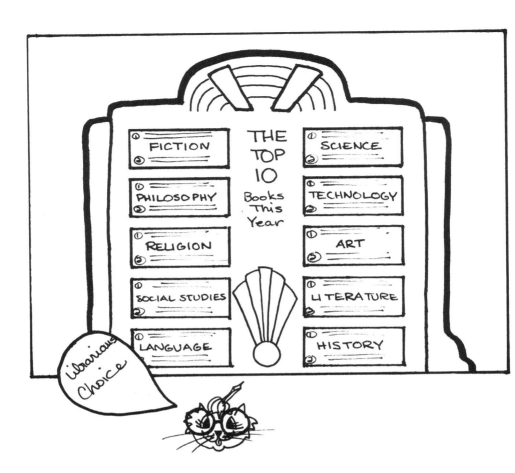

−TOP TEN−

BACKGROUND: None.

LETTERS: Large−white cut-out. Small−black plastic.

METHOD: Using a combination of blue, red, and yellow posterboard, construct a garish jukebox. On white cards, print an author's name and a book title (your selection) in each of the ten categories. Offset the numbers with red posterboard circles.

—LONG ARM OF THE LAW—

BACKGROUND: White paper or fabric.

LETTERS: Black plastic.

METHOD: Place an arm made of construction paper well beyond the center of the board. Give the arm a sand-colored hand, white cuff, and navy pinstripe sleeve. The black academic gown is made with crepe paper. Use a purchased chain, and attach to discs of yellow poster-board. Display with books on good citizenship, hobbies, and various life-filling interests.

—WHY SETTLE FOR HAMBURGER?—

BACKGROUND: None.

LETTERS: Red posterboard cut-out.

METHOD: Fill a bun made from sand construction paper with felt squares as follows: rust and yellow (cheeses), brown (padded to resemble a hamburger), adding touches of red (ketchup). Stuff the bun with green Easter grass between layers (lettuce). Glue real seeds to top of the roll. Display with classics.

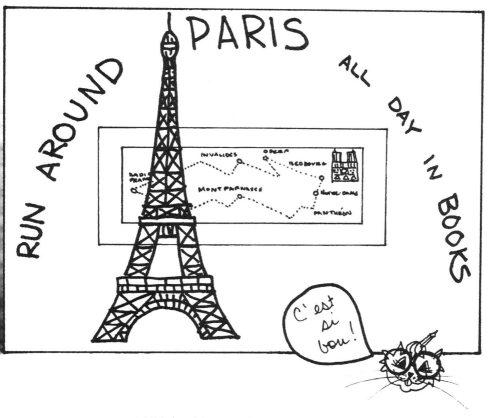

−RUN AROUND PARIS ALL DAY−

BACKGROUND: Light blue paper.

LETTERS: Large−white cut-out. Small−white plastic.

METHOD: With a black felt pen, make a border around a yellow posterboard runner's map; then place names of places on the map. Glue black paper dots or footprints to mark a path. Construct the Eiffel Tower with black yarn and straight pins.

JUNE:

NOW IS THE HIGH TIME OF THE YEAR...

Time to make hay.. .crowding years in one brief moon... exams.. .the Prom.. .when hopes of spring are realized.. .nothing so rare.. .GRADUATION.. .time to break away...

SO LONG, AU REVOIR...GOOD-BYE !

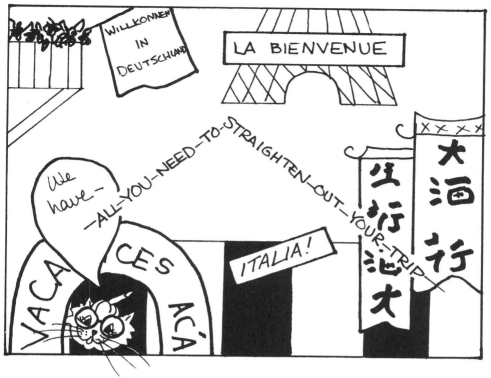

—TRAVELOGUE—

BACKGROUND: None.

LETTERS: Black plastic (forum roofline); cut-out and felt markers.

METHOD: Hang a yellow flag (red lettering) from a balcony made with black posterboard slats and a length of Styrofoam. Red geraniums should spill over the side of the balcony. Cut the Spanish cave from sand posterboard. Construct the forum with white posterboard, and the sign with green posterboard. Make part of the Eiffel Tower with black yarn and straight pins. Chinese flags are made from silk-type fabric lengths, marked in black and suspended from posterboard hangers. Display with dictionaries and guide books. Also, this display is useful as a backdrop to foreign language projects.

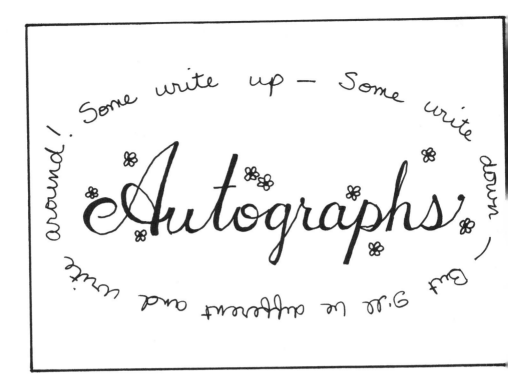

—AUTOGRAPHS—

BACKGROUND: Pink paper.

LETTERS: White cut-out.

METHOD: Decorate the center of the board with paper flowers. Write the verse with purple chalk or marker. Be sure to pencil in the saying first. Display with books of short verse, quotations, and other books that will enhance this year-end activity.

−DISCOVER A FOREIGN WORLD (PASSPORT)−

BACKGROUND: Upper and side sections—white.

LETTERS: Form the word "Official" to resemble a real passport. Cut holes in proportion to the size of your board. Remaining letters are in gold cut-out.

METHOD: Cut a front passport cover from dark green construction paper, and make the back cover from a lighter green.

—MEET HERCULE POIROT—

BACKGROUND: Red paper or fabric.

LETTERS: Black plastic or cut-out.

METHOD: Cut a derby from black construction paper. Fashion a mustache with black yarn.

–FABRICATIONS–

BACKGROUND: Solid fabric with an interesting or unusual texture.

LETTERS: Coordinating colored cut-out.

METHOD: Mount book covers (or facsimiles) on corrugated squares and ovals that have first been covered in a variety of fabrics, i.e., burlap, brocade, calico, or khaki gabardine. Match the title to the fabric. For example, display *Dracula* on black or red satin material. Titles, of course, are all fiction.

—REFLECTIONS ON CHINA—

BACKGROUND: Divide board: top—red paper; bottom—pink paper.

LETTERS: Large—use an oriental lettering style in pink and red cut-out, with reverse placement. Small—black plastic.

METHOD: This simple board can be used to promote material about China in your library.

—LAID BACK LEISURE—

BACKGROUND: None.

LETTERS: Green cut-out.

METHOD: Devise a hammock in macrame, or put one together with fishnet and string. Place an oversized paper cup (with lemon and straws) on a carpet of green grass. To suggest trees, fashion branches and leaves with paper. Cut posterboard book spines in various sizes and colors, and print an author's name and book title on each spine. Stack the titles with absolute disregard to balance, and tack them to the board.

—HEAD FOR A NEW HORIZON—

BACKGROUND: None.

LETTERS: Green cut-out.

METHOD: The hills of the horizon in the foreground are cut from green construction paper. A rolling effect is achieved by using a black pen to place dot arrangements on the hills. Cut the sun, rainbow, track, and train from posterboard and construction paper. Tack black yarn at right angles for a frame effect. Fiberfill, representing clouds in foreground, is sprayed lightly with black paint to appear as engine steam in the background.

—THIS IS THE STUFF—

BACKGROUND: Light blue paper or fabric.

LETTERS: Large—white cut-out. Small—black plastic.

METHOD: On fabric, tack narrow strips of black paper for a coupon cutting line. If you use a paper background, draw these lines with a black marker. Cut an island of green grass carpeting and a palm tree of brown construction paper, with foliage of shredded green tissue paper. Tack blue yarn to simulate the motion of water; use blue lettering in this area.

—BIG PAYOFF—

BACKGROUND: Your school color(s).

LETTERS: Stencil your school's name in gold. Other—use the lighter shade of your school colors in cut-outs.

METHOD: Heap and tack many diplomas (rolled white paper tied with yellow ribbons). Attach a swag of two or three gold cords at the upper-left and upper-right corners of the board. Ribbons of satin or crepe paper in the school colors should hang down each side of the board.

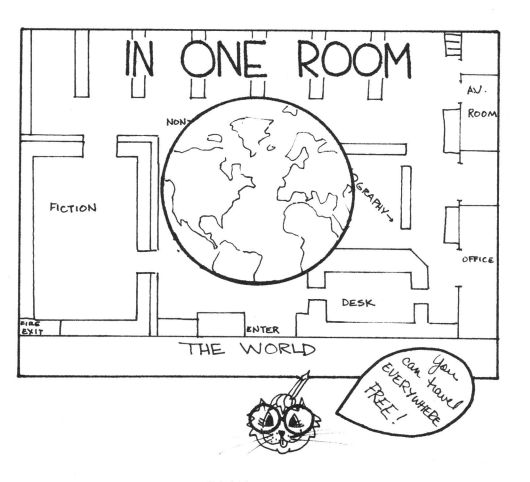

—IN ONE ROOM—

BACKGROUND: White paper.

LETTERS: Blue and yellow cut-out.

METHOD: Using a blue marker, draw a simple floor plan of your library on white background. Superimpose a large picture of the world over this drawing, or hang/tack colorful paper facsimiles of the continental areas.

—SALE IS ON—

BACKGROUND: Light blue paper or fabric.

LETTERS: Dark blue yarn script.

METHOD: Construct a simple sailboat with construction paper. Allow red sails to billow and flags to fly for a three-dimensional effect. Highlight a red sunset with red and gold sparkle string. Use this display to declare a fine-free book return day at the end of the school year.

−LOST ART OF TRAVEL−

BACKGROUND: Light blue paper or fabric.

LETTERS: Large−dark blue cut-out. Small−white plastic.

METHOD: Assemble an ocean liner, *Isle de France*, with dark blue and buff construction paper. Top with a red flag.

–BREAK AWAY THIS SUMMER–

BACKGROUND: Yellow or light blue paper or fabric.

LETTERS: Large–flowered fabric. Small–black plastic.

METHOD: Make a tire with black construction paper and a rim with orange. Use black yarn for spokes. Tack lots of gray paper chains[1] over puffs of smoke made of fiberfill, showing that everything is flying in the wake of the wheel. Feature summer reading for relaxation.

---

[1] Save these from board *Behind Bars*, page 74.

—THREE MEN—

BACKGROUND: Plain or figured fabric in colors appropriate for Father's Day.

LETTERS: Black cut-out.

METHOD: Cut three silhouettes of the male head: two white and one black.[1] Tack an oversized crepe paper bow under the chin of each silhouette.

---

[1] Felson, Henry. *Letters to a Teen-aged Son.*

Shakespeare, William. *Hamlet.* Polonius's speech to Laertes.

Teague, Robert. *Letters to a Black Boy.*

—CONEY ISLAND OF THE MIND—

BACKGROUND: Any appropriate fabric, i.e., a gaudy red and yellow polka dot.

LETTERS: Black plastic.

METHOD: Tack colored streamers at the top and sides of the board to create a tent. Use a child's real clown costume (or make one with paper), gathering ruffs with remaining streamers. Stuff a plastic bag with tissue paper for a head. Stuff the body also if a costume is used. Tack yellow construction paper bars on pictures of circus animals. Display with books on higher math, abstract art, modern poetry, science fiction, and the like.

—SCHOOL MEMORIES—

BACKGROUND: None.

LETTERS: Cut-out in school colors.

METHOD: With pushpins, hang items associated with life in your school, i.e., T-shirts, sports letters, visors, ribbons, and pom-poms. Purchase or make shoebag(s), and fill with shoes that represent school activities (such as dancing or sports shoes, loafers, etc.). An alternative is to collect several pairs of red tennis shoes, ranging in size from toddler to adult.

IT'S ALL OVER NOW. THE END. FINIS. SENIORS, HIGH SCHOOL DAYS WILL SOON BE A THING OF THE PAST. P.S. 123 LIBRARY HAS OFFERED YOU THE WORLD FROM A TO Z. HOPE YOU MAKE THE MOST OF IT'S SERVICES. AND NOW YOU HAVE NEW WORLDS TO CONQUER. SO WHEREVER YOU GO, -TO WORK, OR TO HIGHER COURSES OF LEARNING, ALWAYS REMEMBER WHAT A GOOD FRIEND YOU HAVE IN LIBRARIES EVERYWHERE. EACH STANDS READY TO SERVE YOU WELL IN MORE WAYS THAN YOU CAN EVER IMAGINE NOW. TRUST US.

BEST OF LUCK ALWAYS. --
P.S. 123 LIBRARY

I just hate GOOD-BYES sniff!

—BEST OF LUCK—

BACKGROUND: White paper.

LETTERS: Black and white chalk, or a marker.

METHOD: Make a giant letter "Z" with black construction paper. Print a message in reverse colors: black on white; white on black. Display with brochures from other libraries (college and public) in your area, along with some information on the Library of Congress classification scheme. A limited number of conversion charts can be obtained from the Library of Congress.

—ALWAYS LEAVE 'EM LAUGHING—

BACKGROUND: White paper.

LETTERS: Black and white plastic.

METHOD: Superimpose red construction paper lips over white teeth that have been formed with the aid of a black marking pen. Tack jokes pertaining to libraries and librarians (which you have clipped from magazines over a period of time) to the teeth. Start collecting for this one now.

−GREAT ENTERTAINMENT−

BACKGROUND: White paper.

LETTERS: Red cut-out.

METHOD: Cover a corrugated trapezoid with red checked fabric. Allow some material to overhang at the lower edge. Tack the upper corners of the fabric to the board; brace the lower corners with blocks of Styrofoam. Use coordinating colors for megaphones and pom-poms, folded napkins, and paper plates. Cut away at an angle one-third of each paper cup, and tape in place. Display with books on parties, entertaining, and etiquette.

JULY AND AUGUST:

SUMER IS ICUMEN IN...

Feel it's ripening breath. . .fantastic
heat. . .reel through the days. . .
revel in the nights. . .PLAYTIME. . .
boating. . .fishing. . .golf. . .
reading. . .reflections. . .swimming
. . .tennis. . .touch mountians and
sea. . .all on a summer's day. . .

EAT IT'S CONSECRATED BREAD,
DRINK IT'S IMMORTAL WINE. . .

−THE CIVIL WAR−

BACKGROUND: White paper.

LETTERS: Large−gray on blue cut-out. Small−black plastic.

METHOD: Make two paper flags—one, the Confederate battle flag; the other, the American flag of 1860. Each should be approximately one-half the size of your board. Cut each flag into three pieces, and mount as a collage. Add a silhouette of Lincoln and hats, rifles, or any appropriate symbol that is available.

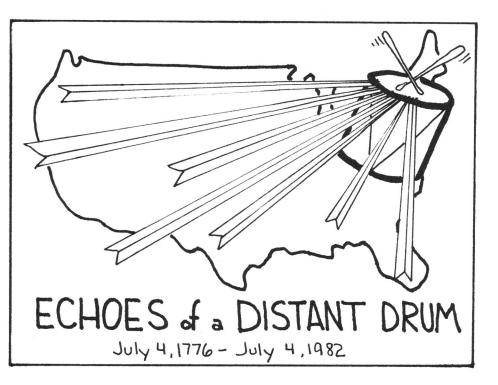

—ECHOES OF A DISTANT DRUM—

BACKGROUND: Red paper or fabric.

LETTERS: Large—white cut-out. Small—white plastic.

METHOD: Enlarge a United States map to desired size on blue construction paper. Red, white, and blue streamers should emanate from a toy drum and drumsticks.

—SUMMER COOLERS—

BACKGROUND: Yellow paper; red counter at lower board is edged with a white posterboard strip.

LETTERS: Blue on green cut-out, and white plastic.

METHOD: Collect several cylindrical boxes in various sizes. Wrap each box in a plastic book cover into which book jackets have been inserted. Top each glass with fiberfill and straws. Add cherries, lemon and lime slices, made with construction paper.

—DON'T GO NEAR THE WATER—

BACKGROUND: Light blue paper or fabric.

LETTERS: None.

METHOD: Proceed from the lower edge of board, and tack green yarn in a scalloped arrangement, diminishing in both color intensity and frequency of line as you approach the top of the board. Cut a large question mark from black construction paper. Use this board to draw attention to books on water safety or water pollution.

—BE SOMEBODY—

BACKGROUND: White paper.

LETTERS: Large—red cut-out. Small—black plastic.

METHOD: Assemble a bassett hound with segments of colored construction paper; cut to scale with the aid of an opaque projector.

—DIP INTO SOMETHING COMFORTABLE—

BACKGROUND: Top third—light blue or aquamarine paper. Lower two-thirds—darker shades of the same color.

LETTERS: Large—white cut-out. Small—white plastic.

METHOD: Cut a buoy and flag from the darker paper, adding a white stripe to the flag. Staple silver sparkle garland along the scalloped edge, placing bits and pieces over the "I's" to indicate water splashes. Display with books or jackets on various water sports.

—JULY 4TH—

BACKGROUND: A collage creation of large pictures of people, places, and/or events associated with the Revolutionary War.

LETTERS: Black plastic or cut-out.

METHOD: Construct a suggestion of a flag over your collage using an arrangement of white stars and white posterboard strips.

−CHILDREN'S HOUR−

BACKGROUND: Black or dark gray paper or fabric.

LETTERS: Large−gray cut-out (note backward spelling). Small−white or black plastic.

METHOD: An easel, placed nearby, holds an appealing picture of children, along with an invitation to a library activity (such as a children's hour or scheduled book talk). Snapshots of previously held library reading activities are useful here, also.

—A LITTLE NIGHT FISHING—

BACKGROUND: Dark blue paper.

LETTERS: Light blue cut-out (apply glitter).

METHOD: Determine a waterline by stapling small amounts of polyester fiberfill to the board. To suggest underwater movement, use soft white chalk and lightly stroke one-inch lines below the fiberfill. Lightly spray fiberfill and chalk marks with glue, then sprinkle with blue glitter. Garden sticks and string represent fishing poles. Tack book jackets under the pier before covering the water area with clear plastic wrap. Tack the black posterboard pier to the board last, placing it over everything else.

—SAVE THE WHALE—

BACKGROUND: Light blue paper.

LETTERS: Felt marker.

METHOD: Cut a whale's tail from black construction paper. Draw lines with blue chalk. Print a posterboard sign, and place it in the hand of a small stuffed animal.

—OYEZ, OYEZ, OYEZ—

BACKGROUND: Yellow paper.

LETTERS: Large—red cut-out. Small—black plastic.

METHOD: Make a parrot with three shades of green construction paper. Cut the breast and tail areas first, fringing strips of lime paper with scissors. Superimpose wings and a head over the figure. Curl pipe cleaner claws over a trapeze made of black posterboard. Outline a white speechframe with a red marker. Feature books that deal with words.[1]

---

[1] Use unusual words, such as quisling, jackanapes, hocus pocus, horsefeathers, enigma, isinglass, and hoosegow.

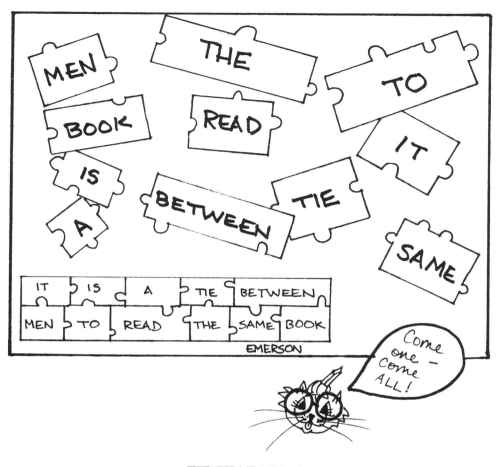

—TIE THAT BINDS—

BACKGROUND: Dark paper or fabric.

LETTERS: Print with felt pen in a coordinating color.

METHOD: Cut puzzle pieces from white posterboard. Post a smaller facsimile of this puzzle nearby, reversing the color scheme. Feature books for which you have duplicate copies.

```
┌─────────────────────────────────────────────────────────┐
│                                                         │
│                                                         │
│                                                         │
│                                                         │
│                                                         │
│                                                         │
│   BOOKS THAT MAKE YOU  SEE RED                          │
│                                                         │
│                                                         │
│                                                         │
│                                                         │
└─────────────────────────────────────────────────────────┘
```

−BOOKS THAT MAKE YOU SEE RED−

BACKGROUND: Red paper or fabric.

LETTERS: Red foil paper, mounted on black.

METHOD: The red background is best left as is to achieve full impact. However, conditions may preclude this arrangement; you may have to tack book jackets (or facsimiles) on the board itself. Use titles dealing with controversial issues.[1]

---

[1] Allen, Thomas B., *Vanishing Wildlife of North America*; Boulle, Pierre, *Face of a Hero*; Clark, Walter, *Ox-Bow Incident*; Costain, Thomas, *Darkness & the Dawn*; Dickens, Charles, *Oliver Twist*; Faulkner, Peter, ed., *Silent Bomb*; Frank, Ann, *Diary*; Griffin, John, *Black Like Me*.

—LONG HOT SUMMER—

BACKGROUND: Cover top third of board with red foil. Superimpose orange construction paper over both foil and remaining board area.

LETTERS: Yellow cut-out.

METHOD: First, determine three arc lines. Next, 1) slash sun rays at top, exposing red foil; 2) attach gold sparkle garland on arc and rays of center sun; and 3) cut flame border from gold foil paper, and tack over larger flames of red foil.

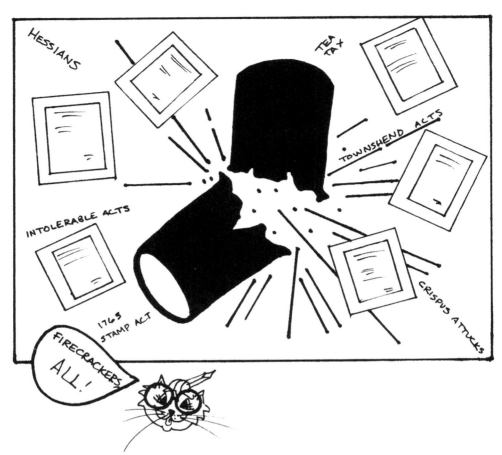

–FIRECRACKERS ALL–

BACKGROUND: White paper.

LETTERS: Black cut-out.

METHOD: Cut a giant firecracker from black construction paper, adding explosion lines of red sparkle string. Mount pertinent book jackets and/or documents on red construction paper squares.

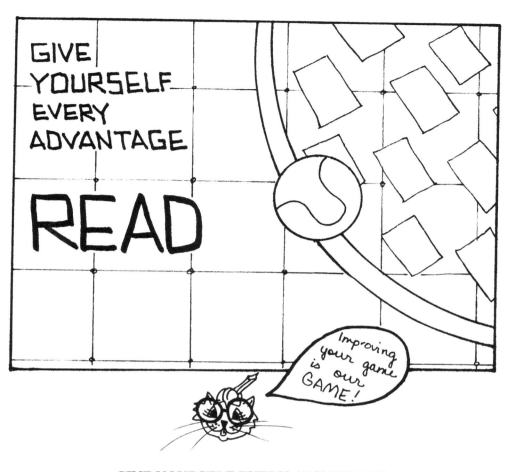

—GIVE YOURSELF EVERY ADVANTAGE—

BACKGROUND: Green paper or imitation grass.

LETTERS: Large—white cut-out. Small—white plastic.

METHOD: Tack three to five lines of white cording across the board horizontally, and pull taut. Repeat the process vertically with four to six lines of cording. Loop or knot at each intersection, forming a net. A racquet is made with shapes cut from sand posterboard. Mount a lime or orange felt circle on a corrugated circle for a tennis ball. Draw lines with a felt marker.

–OUT OF THE DEEP–

BACKGROUND: Dark blue or black paper.

LETTERS: Yellow cut-out.

METHOD: A window is best for this display so letters can hang, and diving gear can be exhibited. Drape purchased fishnet and garlands of imitation greens. Hang Spanish moss, if available. Place shells and books about the sea on a bed of sand (first protecting the floor with a plastic covering).

—COLLECT MORE THAN A TAN—

BACKGROUND: Dark blue paper or fabric.

LETTERS: Yellow cut-out.

METHOD: Tack light blue yarn in a scalloped arrangement across the board. The many segments in the large shell are cut from construction paper of various shades of green, with the darkest shade at the center. Tack (or otherwise display) real shells (perhaps with the aid of masking tape).

—BEACH PARTY PACKAGE—

BACKGROUND: Sand construction paper.

LETTERS: Blue cut-out, the first letter of each word on a varicolored beach ball.

METHOD: Before proceeding, first work out this board with newspaper. Cut a paper visor, tumbler, and feet with tabs, making sure to cut fold-back tabs on the sides of each item to create a three-dimensional effect when mounted. Add fiberfill and straws to a glass, and stack real or mock books.

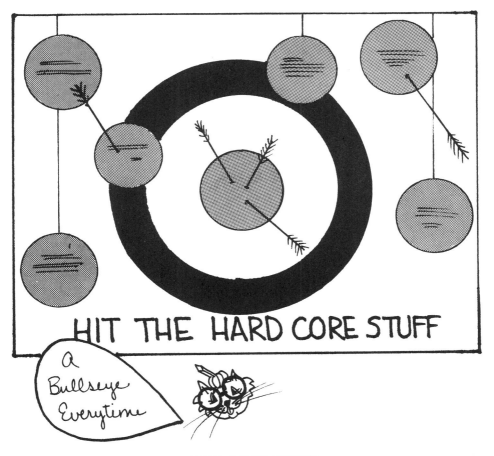

HIT THE HARD CORE STUFF

a Bullseye Everytime

—HARD CORE STUFF—

BACKGROUND: White paper or fabric.

LETTERS: Black cut-out.

METHOD: Make the target flat or three dimensional—the outer circle is of black; middle, white; and inner, red. Cut several red bull's-eyes to hang or tack. On each eye, feature a title about people or movements in history that fulfill the definition of "hard core": an unyielding element in a social organization or structure, i.e., the Amish, women's liberation, Communism, the Klan. Impale toy or paper arrows on the bull's-eyes.

BIBLIOGRAPHY

The books in this listing are some of those that were helpful in the development of many ideas and methods described in this book.

Alkema, Chester Jay. *Greeting Cards You Can Make*. New York, NY: Sterling, 1973.

Angel, Juvenal L., ed. *Directory of Foreign Firms Operating in the U.S.*, 4th ed. New York, NY: World Trade Academy, 1978.

Ballinger, Raymond A. *Lettering Art in Modern Use*. New York, NY: Van Nos Reinhold, 1965.

Barkin, Carol and James, Elizabeth. *Slapdash Decorating*. New York, NY: Lothrop, Lee, & Shepard, 1977.
Wall hangings, curtain ideas, framing. Stimulates creativity.

Bennett, Charles with Taylor, Gerald and Yatabe, Peggy. *Make Your Own Greeting Card Book*. Los Angeles, CA: J. P. Tarcher, 1977. (Dist.: St. Martin's).
Alphabet, Raggedy Ann & Andy, Noah's Ark.

Better Homes & Gardens. *Stitchery & Crafts*. Des Moines, IA: Meredith Corp., 1966.
Pinata, pages 108-109.

Biegeleisen, J. I. *Design and Print Your Own Posters*. New York, NY: Watson-Guptill, 1976.

Brandreth, Gyles. *Biggest Tongue Twister Book in the World*. New York, NY: Sterling, 1978.

Card and Cardboard Colorcrafts. New York, NY: Franklin Watts, 1971.
Animals, hats, and masks.

Cataldo, John W. *Lettering*. New York, NY: Davis Mass, 1958.

Cavanagh, J. Albert. *Lettering and Alphabets*. New York, NY: Dover, 1946.

Cordello, Becky Stevens. *Celebrations*. New York, NY: Butterick, 1977.
Holiday ideas, decorations, and easy craft activities.

Crosbie, John S. *Dictionary of Puns*. New York, NY: Harmony, 1977.

Dodds, Barbara. *Negro Literature for High School Students*. Urbana, IL: National Council of Teachers of English, 1968.

Encyclopedia of American Facts and Dates. Gorton Carruth & Assoc. New York, NY: Crowell, 1972.

Espy, Willard R. *An Almanac of Words at Play*. New York, NY: Potter, 1975. (Dist.: Crown).

Faber, Harold. *Book of Laws*. New York, NY: Times Books, 1979.
Humorous and memorable axioms and aphorisms.

Felton, Bruce and Fowler, Mark. *Best, Worst, and Most Unusual*. New York, NY: Crowell, 1975.

Gardner, Martin. *Mathematical Circus*. New York, NY: Knopf, 1979.
Games, puzzles, and paradoxes from *Scientific American*.

Gordon, Maggie. *Alphabets and Images*. New York, NY: Scribner, 1974.
Inspiration from letterforms.

Graves, Maitland. *The Art of Color and Design*. New York, NY: McGraw, 1951.

Holdgate, Charles. *Netmaking*. Buchanan, NY: Emerson Books, 1972.

Inglefield, Eric. *Flags*. New York, NY: Arco, 1979.

Judge, Clark S. *Best, Worst, Least, and Most: The U.S. Book of Rankings*. New York, NY: Harcourt Brace Jovanovich, 1980.

Kane, Joseph Nathan. *Famous First Facts*. New York, NY: H. W. Wilson, 1964.
Record of events, discoveries, and inventions in the United States.

Katz, Marjorie P. and Arbeiter, Jean S. *Pegs to Hang Ideas On*. New York, NY: M. Evans, 1973.

Laliberté, Norman and Mogelon, Alex. *Silhouettes, Shadows, and Cutouts*. New York, NY: Van Nos Reinhold, 1968.
Ingenious motifs with inexpensive, easily obtained materials.

Leeming, Joseph. *Fun with Greeting Cards*. Philadelphia, PA: Lippincott, 1960.

Littell, Joseph F. *The Comic Spirit*. Rev. ed. New York, NY: Lothrop, Lee, & Shepherd, 1975.

Mann, William. *Lettering and Lettering Display*. New York, NY: Van Nos Reinhold, 1974.

Moncrieffe, Iain and Pottinger, Don. *Simple Heraldry*. New York, NY: Mayflower Books, 1979.

Morrison, Lillian, ed. *Yours Till Niagara Falls*. New York, NY: Crowell, 1950.

Myers, Robert J. *Celebrations*. Garden City, NY: Doubleday, 1972.
Complete book of American holidays.

Newman, Thelma R.; Newman, Jay Hartley; and Scott, Lee. *Paper as Art and Craft*. New York, NY: Crown, 1973.

Nicholsen, Margaret E. *People in Books*. New York, NY: H. W. Wilson, 1969.
Guide to biographical literature arranged by vocations and other fields of reader interest.

Perry, Margaret. *New Christmas Magic*. Garden City, NY: Doubleday, 1975.

Prochnow, Herbert, and Prochnow, Herbert, Jr. *A Treasury of Humorous Quotations*. New York, NY: Harper & Row, 1969.

Purdy, Susan. *Christmas Decorations for You to Make*. Philadelphia, PA: Lippincott, 1965.

Purdy, Susan, 1971. *Costumes for You to Make*. Philadelphia, PA: Lippincott.

Purdy, Susan, 1967. *Holiday Cards for You to Make*. Philadelphia, PA: Lippincott.

Robertson, Patrick. *The Book of Firsts*. New York, NY: Potter, 1974. (Dist.: Crown).
Chronology of a wide range of "firsts," with emphasis on those who have helped alter society in some way.

Salk, Erwin A., comp. *A Layman's Guide to Negro History*. New York, NY: McGraw, 1967.
Books and teaching aids. Includes a list of major events and personalities in the United States.

Schwartz, Alvin. *A Twister of Twists, A Tangler of Tongues*. Philadelphia, PA: Lippincott, 1972.

Seidelman, James E. and Mintonye, Grace. *Creating with Papier-Mache*. New York, NY: Crowell-Collier, 1971.

Selbie, Robert. *Anatomy of Costume*. Los Angeles, CA: Crescent Books, 1977.

Shaw, Harry. *Dictionary of Literary Terms*. New York, NY: McGraw, 1972.

Stephan, Barbara B. *Decorations for Holidays and Celebrations*. New York, NY: Crown, 1978.

Stevenson, Burton. *Macmillan Book of Proverbs, Maxims, and Famous Phrases*. New York, NY: Macmillan, 1948.

Wallechinsky, Irving and Wallechinsky, Amy, comps. *People's Almanac Presents the Book of Lists*. New York, NY: Morrow, 1975.

BIBLIOGRAPHY – BULLETIN
BOARDS – DISPLAYS

Bowers, Melvyn K. *Easy Bulletin Boards*. Metuchen, NJ: Scarecrow, 1974.
Drawings and descriptions: one per page. Introductory chapters on basics, materials, and lettering. Juvenile.

Coplan, Kate. *Effective Library Exhibits*. Rev. 2nd ed. Dobbs Ferry, NY: Oceana, 1974.
Wide scope. Preparation techniques, book fairs, lighting. Circa 95 display ideas. Photos. Bibliography.

Coplan, Kate, 1962. *Poster Ideas and Bulletin Board Techniques*, Dobbs Ferry, NY: Oceana.
Poster creations with instructions in lettering and format. Covers seasons, some holidays, special events, and miscellany. Care of materials and supply sources.

Display: A Handbook of Bulletin Board Ideas, Stevensville, MI: Educational Services, 1975.
Juvenile. How to.

Eisenberg, Larry. *Bulletin Board-ers*, Lima, OH: CSS, 1973.

Fiarotta, Phyllis, and Fiarotta, Noel. *Pin It, Tack It, Hang It: The Big Book of Kids' Bulletin Board Ideas*. New York, NY: Workman, 1975.
Sketches, photos, how-to-make. No index.

Fuda, George E., and Nelson, Edwin L. *The Display Specialist*. New York, NY: McGraw, 1976.
A text-workbook designed to prepare a person to work as a display specialist in retail stores. Good, easy, and practical ideas.

Garvey, Mona. *Library Displays: Their Purpose, Construction, and Use*. New York, NY: H. W. Wilson, 1969.
Mostly text. Very few ideas. Publicity benefits, design elements, lettering, and layout.

Harrison, Pat. *Bulletin Board Ideas*. Cincinnati, OH: Standard, 1977.

Horn, George F. *Bulletin Boards*. New York, NY: Van Nos Reinhold, 1962.

Koskey, Thomas Arthur. *Baited Bulletin Boards: Handbook for Teachers*. San Francisco, CA: Pitman Learning, 1954.

Koskey, Thomas Arthur, 1958. *Bulletin Boards for Holidays and Seasons*. San Francisco, CA: Pitman Learning.

Koskey, Thomas Arthur, 1962. *Bulletin Boards for Subject Areas*. Belmont, CA: Pitman Learning.

McClelland, Tanya A., and Deary, Mary Ann. *Signs of the Times: Bulletin Boards for All Seasons*. Minneapolis, MN: T. S. Denison, 1974.

Miller, Michael M. *Bulletin Boards and Displays: A Bibliography*. Bismark, ND: North Dakota State Library, 1978.

Nuhn, Elizabeth, and Stock, Roma J. *Bulletin Board Bonanza*. Bountiful, UT: Horizon, 1973.

Randall, Reino, and Haines, Edward C. *Bulletin Board and Display*. Worcester, MA: Davis Mass, 1961.
Bibliography.

Robinson, James H., and Robinson, Rowena D. *Bulletin Board Ideas*. St. Louis, MO: Concordia, 1973.

Rowe, Frank A. *Display Fundamentals*. Cincinnati, OH: Signs of Times, 1976.

Ruby, Doris, and Ruby, Grant. *Bulletin Boards for the Middle Grades*. Belmont, CA: Pitman Learning, 1964.
Circa 35 drawings with objectives, suggestions, and instructions for color and construction with patterns.

Sherrod, Sherry. *Displays for Schools: An Avenue of Communication*. Ann Arbor, MI: Displays for Schools, 1977.

Vessel, Matthew F., and Wong, Herbert H. *Science Bulletin Boards*. Belmont, CA: Pitman Learning, 1962.
By month and topic.

Wallick, Clair. *Looking for Ideas?* Metuchen, NJ: Scarecrow, 1970.
Circa 35 full page photos.

SOURCES FOR MATERIALS

Afro-Am Distributing Co. 910 South Michigan Avenue, Chicago, IL 60605.
    Pictures.

American Library Association. 50 East Huron Street, Chicago, IL 60611.
    Library promotionals.

APA Institute, Ltd. 1306 Washington Avenue, St. Louis, MO 63103.
    Lettering. New books on graphic arts—layout.

Appomattox Court House. National Historical Park. Appomattox, VA 24522.
    Civil War memorabilia.

Argus Communications. 7440 Natchez Avenue, Niles, IL 60648.
    Photos of animals and scenes. Most with quips. Under $5.00.

Beckley-Cardy. 114 Gaither Drive, Mt. Laurel, NJ 08054.
    Arts and crafts supplies. Traffic signs and symbols.

Bureau of Engraving and Printing. Office Services Branch. 14th & C Streets, SW,
Washington, DC 20226.
    Black ink engravings: Presidential portraits. Chief Justices. Buildings.

Brodart, Inc. Supply Order Dept. 1609 Memorial Avenue, Williamsport, PA 17705.
    Posters — 19 x 25 — color. Inexpensive.

Caedmon. 1995 Broadway, New York, NY 10023.
    Juvenile posters.

Chicago Sun-Times. 401 North Wabash, Chicago, IL 60611.
    Write Ann Landers here.

Childrens Book Council. 67 Irving Place, New York, NY 10003.
    Bibliographies. Promotional materials.

Collegiate Cap & Gown Co., 1002 North Market Street, Champaign, IL 61820.
    Cap and gown (inexpensive) and pendants.

Documentary Photo Aids. P.O. Box 956, Mount Dora, FL 32757.

Economic Press, Inc. 12 Daniel Road, Fairfield, NJ 07004.
Dennis the Menace profit booster posters.

Encyclopedia Britannica Educational Corp. 425 North Michigan Avenue, Dept. 10A, Chicago, IL 60611.
Study prints.

Footnotes, F. Randolph Assoc., Inc. 1300 Arch Street, Philadelphia, PA 19107.
Boutique: posters, Shakespeare, Broadway, opera, ballet, and films. Catalogue $1.00.

Gaylord. Box 4901, Syracuse, NY 13221.
Lettering. Promotionals.

Giant Photos, Inc. P.O. Box 406, Rockford, IL 61105.
Large selection of posters (16 x 20; 8 x 10; 25½ x 37½): educational, topical, decorative, official NFL, and travel.

Hartco Products Co., Inc. West Jefferson, OH 43162.
Graphic supplies and equipment. Dry transfer lettering.

L. Hartman & Co., Inc. Educational Materials. 2840 Peters Creek Road, Box 6262, Roanoke, VA 24019.
Good variety of paper for bulletin board displays.

Hayes School Pub. Co., Inc. 321 Pennwood Avenue, Wilkinsburg, PA 15221.
Bulletin boards. Posters. Charts. Lettering.

Leswing. P.O. Box 3577. San Rafael, CA 94902.
Good for reading posters and advertising packets.

Library of Congress. Information Office. Washington, DC 20540.
Posters. Art prints.

Library of Congress Card Division. Building 159, Navy Yard Annex, Washington, DC 20541.
Write to this address for LC classification schemes.

Martin Luther King, Jr. Center. 503 Auburn Avenue, NE Atlanta, GA 30312.
Posters and photos. "I have a dream" speech.

National Geographic Society. Department 80, Washington, DC 20036.
Maps. Posters.

Nostalgia. 55 West Twenty-seventh Street, New York, NY 10001.
Jazz and movie posters.

Perfection Form Co. Language Arts. 1000 North Second Avenue, Logan, IA 51546.
Rich source for posters, models, maps (literature), and charts.

Primary Communications. P.O. Box 480, 135 East Pennsylvania Avenue, Southern Pines, NC 28387.
Distributor for *Life* Educational Reprints.

Programmed Language Instruction, Inc. 47-20 Forty-Second Street, Box 4247, Sunneyside, NY 11104.
Posters (39 x 24).

Saturday Evening Post. Heirloom Department. 1100 Waterway Boulevard, Indianapolis, IN 46202.
Norman Rockwell art, including *Four Freedoms*.

School Library Journal. 1180 Avenue of the Americas, New York, NY 10036.
Annual buyers guide. Posters. Promotionals. Giveaways.

Shaffer, Dale E., Library Consultant. 437 Jennings Avenue, Salem, OH 44460.
332 sources of display materials, such as posters, charts, maps, study prints, and pictures. Many items free to teachers and librarians.

Trend Enterprises, Inc. St. Paul, MN 55164.
Bulletin board cut-outs. Letters and borders. Giant posters.

Triton Gallery, Inc. 323 West Forty-Fifth Street, New York, NY 10036.
Theater posters (14x22) and theater graphics (23x46 to 42x84).

United Nations. Publications Unit. World Bank. 1818 "H" Street, NW, Washington, DC 20433.
Charts, maps, speech reprints.

U. N. Publications. Room A–3315. New York, NY 10017.
Flag items, photos, posters.

U.S. Government Printing Office. Assistant Public Printer. Superintendent of Documents. Government Printing Office. Washington, DC 20402.
Ask for: *Consumers Guide to Federal Publications.* (Armed Forces decorations and awards available here; these are life-size).

Upstart Library Promotionals. Box 889. Hagerstown, MD 21740.
Posters. Mobiles. Buttons. Balloons. Animal sit-arounds (3–D, up to 12¾ inches high).

Viking/Penguin Inc. 299 Murray Hill Parkway, East Rutherford, NJ 07013.
Order Jackdaws packets here. Mini-courses in history featuring reproductions of primary source materials.

INDEX